Transforming
Bible
study
WITH
Children

Transforming Bible study WITH Children

A Guide for Learning Together

Patricia W. Van Ness

ABINGDON PRESS

Nashville

TRANSFORMING BIBLE STUDY WITH CHILDREN
A GUIDE FOR LEARNING TOGETHER

This book is printed on acid-free paper.

Library of Congress Cataloging-in-Publication Data

VAN NESS, PATRICIA W., 1925—
    Transforming Bible study with children: a guide for learning together / Patricia W. Van Ness.
    p.   cm.
    Includes bibliographical referenes.
    ISBN 0-687-42502-6 (pbk. : alk. paper)
    1. Bible—Children']s use. 2. Bible—Study. 3. Christian education—Teaching methods. I. Title.
    BS618.V35   1991
    268'.432—dc20   90-45474
                                                                           CIP

MANUFACTURED IN THE UNITED STATES OF AMERICA

To Walter
and all the children
from whom I have learned so much.

Contents

Preface

Transforming Bible Study, written by Walter Wink in 1980 and revised in 1990, is a leader's guide to a creative and transforming method of Bible study. In that book he describes how he came to develop this method and how and why it can be transforming, and introduces the approach and gives guidance on how to use it. It is essentially a "how-to" book on using Transforming Bible Study with adults in a variety of settings. It is important to read Wink's book for a more thorough understanding of the method.

This book is not designed to replace Wink's book for children and youth. My purpose is to share the insights that I have gained from my experiences of over forty years of studying with children and youth in the church. These insights were focused after studying with Wink and using this method with children, youth, and adults for more than a dozen years. If you want to learn to do the method well, there is no substitute for your taking a workshop with Wink and his wife, June Keener-Wink. Their schedule can be obtained from Auburn Theological Seminary, 3041 Broadway, New York, NY 10027.

The scripture quotations in this book are from the New Revised Standard Version. Throughout the book I have used inclusive language for God and for people. Consequently some verbiage will be different from that currently used in scripture. One example is my rendition of the kingdom of God as the Realm of God or God's Realm. The word *kingdom* implies throughout human history an autocratic male ruler. That form of government, current during biblical times, is not relevant in Western experience and thought patterns today, and is extant only in places like Iran. The word *realm* implies a sphere of influence and authority.

Chapter 1 sets forth my basic premise that unless you become as a little child, you shall not enter the Realm of God. Consequently, Christian Education needs transformation and a new paradigm in which students and teachers become learners together.

Chapter 2 describes how to use Transforming Bible Study (TBS) to "get the gospel in your gut" so that the transformative process can take place. How to prepare a lesson in this mode and adapt it for use with children and youth is described, and examples of proven experiences are given.

Chapter 3 deals with many of the "if-only-we-had . . ." problems that face any church school. It describes how to work with TBS to transform the way and the setting in which you teach.

Chapter 4 explains why I don't do pageants and describes how you can use this Bible study method as a basis for alternative and innovative ways for children to be involved creatively in worship.

There simply are not words to express my heartfelt appreciation to all the children I have studied with who have taught me so much. Many of these experiences are delineated in this book. Thank you especially Glen Evans, Nicki Lewin, Zak and Yarrow Wright, Mary Boucher, Katie Bean, and all the other unnamed children and youth who participated in meaningful ways in my church school classes.

Thank you Bob Meyer, Louis Woodham, Deidre Lewin, Donald D. M. Jones, Verena Wirz, Don and Charlotte Addiss, and Liane Measell, who supported and encouraged me when some people in their churches thought I was crazy.

Thank you Margaret Bean, Barbara and Chandler W. Gilbert, and Mary Elizabeth McClellan for reading, critiquing, and supporting me in the writing of this book. Thank you, Clyde Slicker and Cheryl Burrows for the information and material on self-esteem. Many thanks to Paul Franklyn, my editor at Abingdon Press, who so graciously shepherded me through this publication process.

Especially thank you, Peter, Stephen, and Timothy Van Ness, for your support and encouragement to write this book; June Keener-Wink for your wonderfully creative crafts and movement, many of which I have utilized; Walter Wink—teacher, mentor, and friend—for years of exciting TBS study and the wisdom, guidance, and encouragement that made this book possible; and most of all, John Van Ness—husband, confidant, supporter, and friend—who encouraged me to write this book in the first place. To all who read and risk trying something new, blessing and peace . . . and enjoy!

Patricia W. Van Ness

Walter Wink

For years, people have been asking me whether the approach I use to Scripture would work with children. I had to admit that I have never tried it with children younger than twelve years old. But I could always point them to Pat Van Ness, who had, and with remarkable success. Now she has drawn together the fruits of a long career as Christian educator, curriculum writer, and friend to children in this book.

Her approach differs not just in method from the way the vast majority of teaching is done, but also in its presuppositions. The ruling assumption here is that children have not only the capacity but also the need to discover the truth for themselves. Christian education should not just be a process of socializing children into Christian values, but also of exorcising the false values of the dominant culture. This requires something seldom taught younger children: the capacity for critical, independent thought. That is the great gift of a genuinely open, questioning method.

Questioning is empowerment. It teaches children how to think—something I was never taught in all my schooling all the way through the Ph.D. It builds a child's confidence that she or he has the capacity to discover truth. How different from the memorize-and-test philosophy that dominates our schools, where one's self-esteem grows by getting grades—that is, by pleasing the teacher through regurgitating what the teacher believes is important.

To teach this way requires that the teacher also undergo the same process as the child: empowerment to discover truth for oneself, learning to think, living in the openness of the questions. What makes this approach so exciting and rewarding is that the teacher also undergoes the process of transformation in the very process of teaching.

Somehow that seems very right, very embedded in the gospel. Perhaps that is because the method itself, and not just what we teach through it, bears witness to the inbreaking of the reign of God.

Transforming
Bible
study
WITH
Children

Chapter 1
"Unless You Become . . ."

What Did Jesus Mean?

When parents tried to bring their children to Jesus for his blessing, the disciples reprimanded them. But Jesus said: "Let the little children come to me, and do not stop them; for it is to such as these that the [Realm] of God belongs. Truly I tell you, whoever does not receive the [Realm] of God as a little child will never enter it" (Luke 18:16-17). What is it about children that makes them able to respond to Jesus and to the Realm of God?

Why did Jesus answer the disciples' question in Matthew 18:1 of who was the greatest in the Realm of God the way he did? What is the childlike humility that Jesus pointed to as a sign of greatness?

On the way to Capernaum, the disciples were having a conversation about who was greatest among them. When they arrived at the house where Jesus was staying, he asked them about their discussion. By their silence he knew what the topic of conversation had been. So he said, "Whoever wants to be first must be last of all and servant of all" (Mark 9:35). Then he took a child in his arms and said, "Whoever welcomes one such child in my name welcomes me; and whoever welcomes me welcomes not me but the one who sent me" (Mark 9:37). How is welcoming a child in Jesus's name being a true servant of God and welcoming Jesus and God?

Many parents seem to assume that the church school has taken the place of Jesus. Therefore, they bring their children to be "blessed"; or more accurately, to be taught the Bible stories so that they will be good, moral, Christian children. However, I believe, as do many other Christian educators, that children understand what Jesus meant, that they intuitively know that other reality that Jesus calls the Realm of God so that even small children have an innate wisdom and a natural closeness with God. As Wordsworth suggests in "Intimations of Immortality":

> Not in entire forgetfulness,
> And not in utter nakedness,
> But trailing clouds of glory do we come
> From God, who is our home:
> Heaven lies about us in our infancy!

The numinous sense of "heaven," or the Realm of God, experienced by children, though not necessarily remembered and verbalized only with difficulty, gives them an awareness of the transcendent reality that is in the world around them. This innate wisdom enables them to have a sense of the meaning of Scripture. Over the years a growing number of educators have been convinced, and my experience tells me, that children as young as five can do perceptive Bible study and arrive at a level of understanding that far exceeds what educators deem "age appropriate."

Doing Bible Study at Worship

One Sunday my husband was leading worship and asked me to do the children's sermon at the church where we regularly worship. The Gospel was Mark 9:33-37. Rather than preach *at* children (which doesn't work), my style is to talk *with* them. Therefore, my task was to see what the children would do with the basic story of Jesus' "calling the children," as it is usually referred to in church-school terms.

Our congregation is made up largely of retired people. There are very few young families. Upon getting up from my pew and looking around, I realized that only Yarrow, ten, and Zak, thirteen, were there. I asked them by name whether they would be willing to come up front. I explained that I wanted to talk with them, not at them, and I wanted their wisdom. They sat in the front row, and I knelt in front of them, so I was the same height. In response to my inquiry "Do you know the story of Jesus' welcoming the little children," they nodded. With some drawing out, they gave me the basics of the story. In response to my question "What do you think the disciples said when the children came?" they were obviously trying to remember what the Bible said. To move them beyond that, my next question was "What do you think the disciples might have said?"

They answered, "Go away." "You can't be here." They smiled at my suggestion, "Scram, kids!" and nodded.

"Do you remember what Jesus said to the disciples?" I asked them. It was obvious they were again searching for the exact biblical words, but they did remember that Jesus wanted the children there. Then I asked, "Do you think the children wanted to be there? Why did Jesus want them there?" Yarrow, with an ineffable smile and an ingenuous shrug of her shoulders, said, "Because they knew that the kingdom of God was where they wanted to be!" Nodding in appreciation, I left a silent space.

"Jesus said that unless we become as a little child we will not enter the kingdom of God. I don't think most adults understand that at all. I'm not really sure I do, and I want your wisdom as to why he said that and what he meant." We batted that question around a bit, going with ideas and words like *responsive* and *willing to learn.* My most profound recollection is that Zak said, "They haven't been corrupted yet." Yarrow said, "They're open."

"Are you saying that children are still open, willing to learn and responsive to new ideas?" I asked. They smiled a "you-got-it" smile, gave me affirmative nods, and said "Yes!" I said, "Thank you. Go in peace."

Uncorrupted—by adults' theology and biblical interpretation? Open and responsive—to the Scripture, to Jesus, to new ideas? Willing to learn—new ways of looking at things? Is that what Jesus meant by humility appropriate for greatness in God's Realm? Is that what enables us to be true servants, assuming last place and ending up first? To receive Jesus and God into our lives? How would these perceptions transform our Bible study, not only in our own study and preparation but also in the church school classroom?

A New Paradigm for Christian Education[1]

Studying the Scripture and sharing our faith *with* and *as* children would alter radically the way we do Christian education. As Westerhoff and Wink suggest, our present way of doing Christian education and Bible study requires a radical reformation.

The intent of Christian education is to provide faith development and to awaken to consciousness the spiritual awareness of people of all ages and all levels of maturity. That requires an intuitive, affective,[2] right-brained,[3] experiential mode of learning. For a number of years some Christian educators have been writing about the necessity of teaching from this perspective rather than from a school-system way of learning: a cognitive, rational, left-brained, linear/logical mode.

In 1976, John Westerhoff commented that although church educators may admit "that learning takes place in many ways" they have "equated the context of education with schooling and the means of education with formal instruction." The model has come from the public school, and the guidelines have come from "secular pedagogy and psychology." The norm has included "teachers, subject matter, curriculum resources, supplies, equipment, age-graded classes, classrooms" and even "a professional church educator. All this," he says, "must change."

Westerhoff questions the purpose of "schooling and instruction." He suggests that the uniqueness of religious education is found in Jesus' question "When the Son of Man comes, will he find faith on earth?" (Luke 18:8). "Surely he will find religion (institutions, creeds, documents, artifacts, and the like)" Westerhoff asserts, "but he may not find faith." Religion, he suggests, "is important, but not ultimately important." From the point of view of Christian education "religion is a means not an end; faith is the only end. Faith, therefore, and not religion, must become the concern of Christian education." Consequently he concludes "that the schooling-instructional paradigm is bankrupt."[4]

Despite the fact that such ideas have been consistently repeated and a more experiential mode of education suggested by some educators, most church school curricula are still too closely tied to that public school paradigm. They are locked into a theory of "age appropriateness," based on educational developmental theory and on Kohlberg's and Fowler's moral and faith development theories (see p. 30). The experiential-learning theory, which Westhoff and others have explicated, has not penetrated to curriculum producers. Nor has it trickled down to the lay teacher in the classroom, who still depends on finding the "right answer" to the "meaning" of biblical passages in the curriculum guide/teacher's book and on Bible storybooks and leaflets to get through a lesson.

The "experiential" mode of learning does not mean for us not to use our minds or for us to throw out our Bible dictionaries, commentaries, atlases, Greek and Hebrew texts, and continuing, scholarly textual research and criticism. Rather, we need to take a good look at what we are trying to accomplish and decide whether or not the method we are using is working before we can work with a more effective approach.

Educational Theory and Implications

Consequently, we need to look at the different ways in which people of all ages learn, what are the most affective ways of communicating facts and eliciting insights and, ultimately, of making the Bible and all these various ways of approaching Christian education relevant to people's lives.

Much research has been done for fifteen to twenty years on the right/left brain learning modes. If the whole person is to be educated, then both sides of the brain need to be taken into account. (See the diagram on p. 20.) Because of the plasticity of the brain, especially among children up to twelve years old, it has "an enormous capacity to reorganize itself," suggesting that "experience can greatly influence and shape the brain development of the child."[5] As in other areas, what children *experience* in church school has more affect on awakening their spiritual awareness than what they *learn*. Since spiritual awareness comes especially from meditation and is perceived in an intuitive manner, right-brain activities are more important than left-brain perception.

Most school curricula, including that for church school, "tend to suppress the holistic, simultaneous, and intuitive mode of consciousness" where spiritual awareness is developed.[6] Such awareness needs the affective domain, which "involves values, emotions, and attitudes."[7] Since faith development and spiritual awareness deal with values, emotions, and attitudes, the use of techniques that develop the right brain are again important. Basing

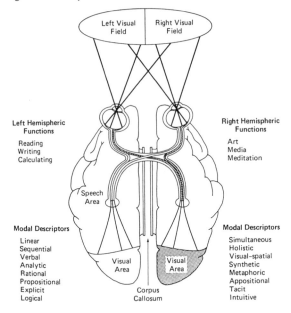

From *Teaching and Brain Research: Guidelines for the Classroom.*
Copyright Michael P. Grady. Used by permission.

her theories on left/right brain research, Bernice McCarthy has
come up with *The 4 Mat System: Teaching to Learning Styles with
Right/Left Mode Techniques,* describing learning style characteris-
tics in four major ways.[8]

Type One persons are the Imaginative Learners who learn by
listening and sharing ideas. They are creative thinkers who believe
in their own experience. They get information from insight/
intuition and process it reflectively. They need to be personally
involved. They seek meaning and clarity. They are interested in
people and culture. Their strengths lie in imaginative ideas, and
they function by value clarification. Their goals are to be involved in
important issues and to bring harmony. Their favorite question is
"Why?"

Type Two persons are the Analytic Learners who devise theories
by integrating their observations into what is known. They need to
know what the experts think. They learn by thinking through ideas.

They need details and facts. They enjoy traditional classrooms and find ideas fascinating. Their strength is in creating concepts and models, and they function by thinking things through. Their goal is intellectual recognition, and their favorite question is "What?"

Type Three persons are the Common Sense Learners. They are pragmatists who learn by testing theories and applying common sense. They believe that if it works use it, and they are down-to-earth problem solvers who resent being given answers. Being skills-oriented, they experiment and tinker with things because they need to know how things work. Their strength is the practical application of ideas. Their goal is to bring their view of the present in line with future security. They function by factual data gathered from hands-on experience, and their favorite question is "How does this work?"

Type Four persons are the Dynamic Learners who learn by trial and error, integrating experience and application. They are believers in self-discovery who are enthusiastic about new things. They are adaptable, relish change, and excel when flexibility is needed. They are risk takers who are at ease with people. They thrive on action and challenges. They function by acting, testing, and creating new experiences. Their goal is to bring action to ideas, and their favorite question is "What if?"—and I would add "So what?"

It appears that much of the public, and even the private, school system is oriented toward Type Two persons—Analytic Learners. Yet, 70 percent of the students are not Analytic Learners. McCarthy suggests that we need to learn in all four ways:

> We sense and feel, we experience
>   then we think, we develop theories, we
> conceptualize;
>   then we try out our theories, we
>   experiment;
>   finally, we apply what we
>   have learned.[9]

When looking at this paradigm of learning from the church school perspective, we could paraphrase the four ways:

> We read, feel into, experience and act out the Bible story;
>> then we think about the social situation
>> and explain what Jesus said or did and why;
>>> then we express our understanding
>>> in drama, crafts, poetry, movement;
>>>> then we talk about and express
>>>> how that is relevant to our
>>>> lives today.

In the Christian education of children and youth, where the goal is faith development and spiritual awareness, analytic learning is the least effective method, whereas the intuitive (Type One) and the dynamic (Type Four) are the most affective. For children, the ultimate theological questions are "Why?"; "What if"; and "So what?" Meaning in life is not derived from knowing the answers but from living the questions.

Rainer Maria Rilke—the poet, story writer, and dramatist—in answering a young, beginning poet who had written for his advice, Rilke admonished him to try to "love the *questions themselves.*" The poet was too young to be able to live the answers, so there was no point in his seeking them. Rather the point was to live everything: "*Live* the questions now. Perhaps you will then gradually, without noticing it, live along some distant day into the answers."[10]

Unfortunately, in the church school we are learning with children who are so programmed by the school system that they are primarily concerned with giving the right answer. Some children find it very difficult to speculate about why Jesus said what he said or to wonder how Jesus might have felt or to delve into the reactions of the disciples, the authorities, the people he encountered. They assume that the "answers" are learned or are in the stories.

In a large urban church, I asked a youth class, aged twelve to fourteen, a why-do-you-think question about the scripture we were studying. One very bright twelve-year-old boy answered my question with a very traditional, parroted, "church-school" answer. Acknowledging his response by smiling and nodding at him, I asked the question again. He nearly exploded, "That's the right answer isn't it?" My reply was, "I don't care whether that's the right answer

CHILDREN LEARN THROUGH DOING

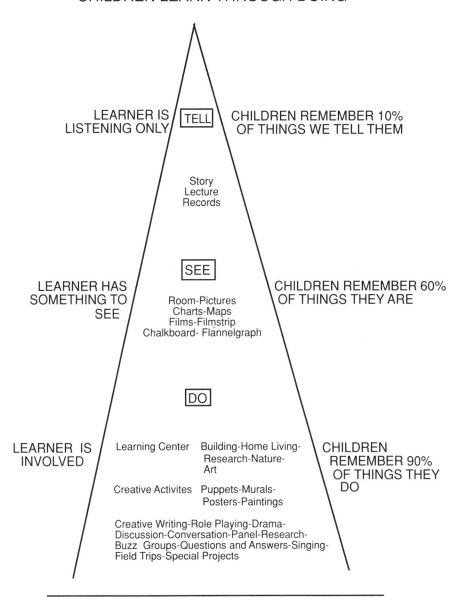

LEARNER IS LISTENING ONLY

TELL

CHILDREN REMEMBER 10% OF THINGS WE TELL THEM

Story
Lecture
Records

SEE

LEARNER HAS SOMETHING TO SEE

Room-Pictures
Charts-Maps
Films-Filmstrip
Chalkboard- Flannelgraph

CHILDREN REMEMBER 60% OF THINGS THEY ARE

DO

LEARNER IS INVOLVED

Learning Center   Building-Home Living-
                   Research-Nature-
                   Art

Creative Activites   Puppets-Murals-
                      Posters-Paintings

Creative Writing-Role Playing-Drama-
Discussion-Conversation-Panel-Research-
Buzz Groups-Questions and Answers-Singing-
Field Trips-Special Projects

CHILDREN REMEMBER 90% OF THINGS THEY DO

From *Teaching and Learning with Older Elementary Children,* by Arlene J. Ban. Copyright © 1979 by Judson Press. Used by permission.

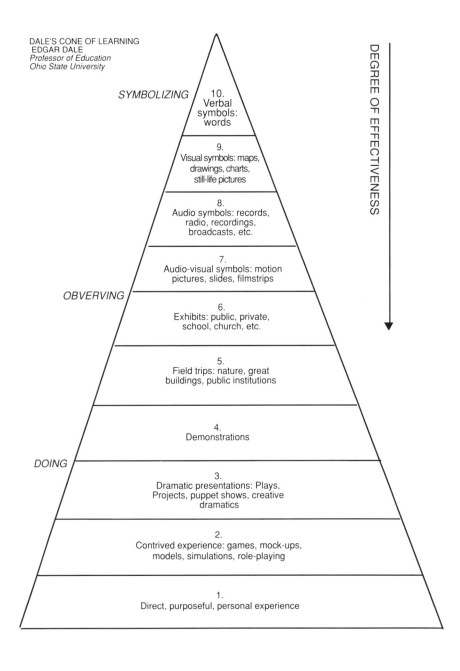

DALE'S CONE OF LEARNING
EDGAR DALE
Professor of Education
Ohio State University

DEGREE OF EFFECTIVENESS

SYMBOLIZING

10.
Verbal symbols: words

9.
Visual symbols: maps, drawings, charts, still-life pictures

8.
Audio symbols: records, radio, recordings, broadcasts, etc.

7.
Audio-visual symbols: motion pictures, slides, filmstrips

OBVERVING

6.
Exhibits: public, private, school, church, etc.

5.
Field trips: nature, great buildings, public institutions

4.
Demonstrations

DOING

3.
Dramatic presentations: Plays, Projects, puppet shows, creative dramatics

2.
Contrived experience: games, mock-ups, models, simulations, role-playing

1.
Direct, purposeful, personal experience

or not, I want to know what *you* think." That totally lost him, and much of the class. The unsaid message was "If you're going to make it in school you have to know the right answer. Don't confuse me with what I think!"

When I wrote church school curriculum for grades one and two using the Transforming Bible Study method, my editor underlined in red some of my questions and wrote, "Children can't answer questions you haven't given them the answer to in the Bible Story Book."

To the contrary, Madeline L'Engle, author of award-winning children's books and writer-in-residence at the Cathedral of St. John the Divine, commented in an interview, "Don't answer questions children haven't asked."

A Paradigm for Transformation

The following diagrams provide a framework for understanding and applying TBS through a better paradigm for Christian education.[11] Notice in Ban's diagram that children remember 10 percent of things we tell them and 90 percent of things they do. In Dale's Cone of Learning the least effective method is words—that is, hearing, reading, writing—and the most effective is direct, purposeful, personal experience. As the Chinese sage Confucius said:

Tell them and they'll forget
Demonstrate and they'll remember
Involve them and they'll understand

From a practical standpoint, being involved in the church school so that personal transformation happens means:

take the chairs out from around the table;
push the table against the wall
put the chairs in a circle for Bible study, sharing, discussion;
use the table(s) for displays, research, ongoing projects;
get the children actively involved by acting out Scripture;
sing, dance, move, do choral readings;
express creatively through murals, poems, puppet/video shows, skits
    an understanding of the Scripture;
discuss, create a project that expresses what all you have done today
    means;
provide opportunities for silence, listening, and an encounter with
    God.

Unfortunately, leaders may complain, "I can't do that!" Except for the unusual, creative, innovative person, most people who volunteer to "teach" will try to replicate their church school experience. With no real understanding of faith development and spiritual awareness as the purpose of Christian education, with limited experiences of their own spirituality and with little or no training, all they can do is to replicate their own experiences. My frustration here is that what they tell me about their church school experience often was irrelevant then and is even more irrelevant now.

College faculty who supervise student teachers express exasperation that no matter what students learn in class about meaningful educational practices, when they get into the local classroom for practice teaching they revert to type and teach the way they were taught even when it was terrible.

At an enlightening conference titled "Creating Our Future in Education," in Bellingham, Washington, innovative educators came from all over the world. Bernice McCarthy, one of the speakers, asked, "How many of you liked school when you were a kid?" About 75 percent of the people raised their hands. Then she asked, "How many of you are now school teachers?" The same 75 percent raised their hands. Next she asked, "How many of you disliked school when you were a kid?" About 15 percent of the people raised their hands. "How many of you are now school teachers?" No one raised a hand.

We teach the way we were taught unless we have had some kind of transforming educational and spiritual experience. That's why there has to be a new paradigm, a new way of looking at Christian education, a basic change in our understanding of what we are about and how we are about that.

What we are about, it seems to me, is no less than being involved in a process of transformation. As we study the Scripture with others, we encounter God through those persons whose encounters with God were recorded in the Bible. If we can live into these stories, into these experiences, we can recapture some of the sense of God's activity in the lives of these persons and see how it relates to our lives today. Since young children especially have few preconceptions about meaning and theology, they can help us to see that freshly, as though for the first time.

If we will then allow ourselves to be right-brained for a while in response to these encounters, we can experience the power of God, the reconciling love of Christ Jesus, and the energy of the Holy Spirit moving in the depths of our beings. If we are willing to risk and allow this to happen, we will experience the transcendent power of the Creator and the whole of the creative universe at work in our lives. But we must be childlike in our receptivity, or we will filter it out with our rational minds. We, like Adam and Eve in the Garden of Eden, will respond in fear to what we learn; we will hide from God and alienate ourselves anew from our loving Creator Parent. It takes great courage to be willing to encounter God in the depth of our beings.

Following his encounter on the Damascus Road, the Apostle Paul became a great "professor" in a new way. Basing a concept of education on Paul's first letter to the church at Corinth (I Cor. 2:1-16), Parker Palmer comments: "Paul's contrast between Spirit filled teaching and the sophistic wisdom of his day can easily be applied to the rationalism which dominates the academic culture in our day." He points out that a professor was someone "who professed a faith," and he suggests: "Great teachers . . . will be living witnesses to the faith that there is a place to stand when the ground gives way beneath one's feet."[12]

"For Paul, maturity is not a matter of having 'the answers. . . . ' The wise person would seem to be one who recognizes the inadequacy of conventional wisdom, the hollowness of popular conceptions of truth. The beginning of wisdom, for Paul, is not answering but questioning."[13] He suggests that there may be a clue here about the problem of answering a question that hasn't been asked: "The root meaning of the word 'education' is 'to draw out. . . . ' Giving answers very seldom draws people out, but questions do."[14]

Palmer also comments that for the Apostle Paul right teaching is "reverence, not power. And reverence means respect for all life, knowing that all men and women are gifted by God, and all are loved."[15] That is certainly also true for children—and for all creatures on this planet.

A New Three R's

Similarly, the new paradigm might also consist of a new set of the three R's that are particularly relevant to Christian education. In *Transforming Education*, Andy LePage outlines an educational theory based on a spiritual orientation. He suggests that what is needed as a basis for curricula are *reverence, renewal,* and *responsibility.*[16] It is a cosmic, rather than a human, understanding of education, similar to that of the Apostle Paul.

We are humans created in the image of God, living on the "visited planet" in which God incarnated in Jesus, the Christ Consciousness, the image of what humanity was intended to be. As we study the scriptures, we see how God has related to us from creation through the early church. Our emphasis is usually on how we respond and how we are related to God. But particularly as we enter the Third Millennium we need to be aware of our cosmic relationships as well.

We need to have *reverence* for the whole of God's creation. We need to have reverence for one another, as fellow human beings created in God's own image. If we treat other people, and especially children and young people, with reverence and respect, they will return that. If we are committed to learning with and from them, we are expressing reverence for the Christ consciousness living within them. And as we talk about God's creation, we need to have reverence for all that God has made.

"*Renewal* happens in education when knowledge and ideas are brought together in such a way as to be made fresh."[17] The book of Revelation reminds us, "See, I am making all things new" (Rev. 21:5). And Paul admonishes us, "Do not be conformed to this world, but be transformed by the renewing of your minds, so that you may discern what is the will of God" (Rom. 12:2). Are we willing to approach a Scripture passage in a new way, a fresh way? Could we get excited about the same old stuff? Are we willing to open our minds to renewal so as to be transformed?

There is much talk today about renewal in the church, but what I hear sounds as though people simply want to get people back into the church without doing enough about why they left in the first place. Many church leaders don't even want to hear why those persons left. For Christian education that means you cannot go on teaching the way you were taught and expect transformation to happen. If your curriculum consists only of listening to the story, filling in the blanks, coloring the picture, learning a Bible verse, and saying a rote prayer, it needs renewal.

What does it mean to have *responsibility* for those whom we teach? Some would say it means to teach them morals and how to be "good Christians," to be responsible for their moral development by telling them how to behave. But how much do students retain of what they hear? About 10 percent. Morals are best taught by example. One of the perennial complaints of young people is that their parents and teachers say, "Do what I say, not what I do."

It seems more responsible for us to provide a learning situation in which children experience how to find out for themselves, to be responsible for their own spiritual growth and faith development, to give them the tools with which to respond to Scripture. We can provide learning experiences that are stimulating, varied, open-ended, alive, and fun. As teachers our responsibility is not to give them the answers, but to help them discover how to live the questions.

From the very beginning God gave us responsibility for this planet and all that lives in it. To have "dominion" (see Gen. 1:26) means to rule over and, therefore, to be responsible for and, consequently, to think ecologically.[18] We simply cannot go on polluting, destroying forests and the ozone layer, and not respecting other creatures. Every five minutes another species becomes extinct because of our lack of awareness. It takes cosmic consciousness to be aware of how we destroy and pollute. That has enormous consequences for how we teach. When the creation story and stewardship are taught in church school, is ecology a basic part of the curriculum?

Self-esteem

The emphasis on right answers in public and church school education has also contributed to a loss of self-esteem in our children. By teaching responsibly, we can recover the respect and attention of children. The position statement on developmentally appropriate practice on the primary grades by the National Association for the Education of Young Children states: "When schools unduly rely on competition and comparison among children, they . . . lessen children's optimism about their own abilities and school in general, and stifle motivation to learn."[19] Conversely, by nurturing their self-esteem we enhance children's ability to learn. "One of the first steps in developing children's self-esteem is to establish . . . relationships that are mutually loving and caring, honest, and supportive (and) create an atmosphere for healthy human growth."[20] The suggestions that seem particularly relevant to church school leadership are

Create an atmosphere of trust by the tone of your voice, by kneeling and speaking to each child at eye level.

Keep questions open-ended.

Be nonjudgmental—the more sensitive you are to each child's feelings the safer she or he will feel.

Provide opportunities for success.

Additionally, in "Children's Self-Esteem: The Verbal Environment," it is noted that adults create a positive verbal environment when they show warmth, acceptance, respect and empathy.[21] Of particular relevance to church school teaching are the suggestions that adults use words that show affection for children and sincere interest in them:

teachers listen attentively to what children have to say;
adults use children's interests as a basis for conversation; and
teachers avoid making judgmental comments about children.

Treating the children with respect enhances their self-esteem more than anything else. There seems no better way to assure this kind of adult leadership in the classroom than to remember the importance of *sharing and learning with children,* rather than trying to teach them something they may not be ready or able to hear or learn. Assuming, therefore, that they do have spiritual awareness and the ability to do Bible study, we may lead them into an encounter with the Bible through questions, listening, and responding to their insights and by sharing faith, which will give the children an unusual sense of their own self-worth.

The place to begin, ultimately, is with ourselves. If we are responsible for our own continuing education, faith development, spiritual awareness so that we have a meaningful relationship with God and with people in our community, an interest in encountering Scripture and letting it encounter us, and some kind of regular spiritual discipline that enriches us, then we will be enabled to share that with others.

Faith Development Theory and Implications

The development of faith has been discussed at length by James W. Fowler in *Stages of Faith* and in *Becoming Adult, Becoming Christian.*[22]

Fowler takes a developmental approach based on the work of Kohlberg.[23] Fowler assumes six stages, beginning at birth and going through death, each developing at an "appropriate age." A growing body of literature challenges Fowler's developmental theories.[24] My problem with this approach is based on my experience with young children who are in a much more advanced stage of spiritual awareness than many adults and far beyond what is considered their appropriate age level. There are also adults who are stuck at what is assumed to be an adolescent level.

When our granddaughter Eva was about two and one half years old, Peter, Nancy, and Eva came from Massachusetts to California to visit us. We had not seen much of Eva, since she was born while we were in California. Sunday after worship we had some people in to dinner, and as our custom was, we held hands and had a silent prayer that lasted several minutes. Eva was very quiet, and when we opened our eyes she was looking at me with a beautiful, ethereal expression, obviously moved by the sense of the Spirit that was in that gathering.

The next evening when we had our silent prayer before dinner, she again was quiet. Afterward, with an awed smile, she said, "Do that again!" And we did. Even at that young age she was well aware of the presence of the Spirit.

Westerhoff's paradigm in *Will Our Children Have Faith?* is to see Christian education as "*a community of faith enculturation*—interactive experiences among people of all ages," sharing "the various ways we strive to be Christian together within a community of faith." He deplores the belief expressed in much Christian education that "human beings are only minds" with the emphasis on intellectual activities, and he calls for a greater emphasis on the intuitional. In Christian education we need to "wonder and create; to dream and fantasize, imagine and vision; to sing, paint, dance and act . . . recover our ecstasy . . . a sensual and kinesthetic awareness . . . and to express ourselves emotionally and nonverbally."[25]

Faith development does not happen through an instructional mode of learning. Hearing the biblical stories and learning about the various biblical characters; being able to repeat the stories; knowing about Jesus' life, death, and resurrection; and being able to say the Ten Commandments, the Lord's Prayer, and the

Beatitudes does not make us disciples. It happens when we encounter the biblical people within their situations by living into them, experiencing some of what they were experiencing, and seeing how that applies to our life today. "The quality of our faith will always reveal what we *are*" suggests Westerhoff. "And what we *are* will in the end determine the value and effect of what we do."[26]

Basing curricula for faith development on the school/didactic/instructional model doesn't work. The model we might be using is that of the guidance counselors in the public school systems. Basically their purpose is to help the children deal with their problems so that they can get beyond them to a place where they can learn.

Cheryl Burrows, a guidance counselor and coordinator for a local school district, explains that much of what she does is preventative. By helping children and youth to develop guidelines for living, to refine and use communication skills, and to acquire decision-making skills, she helps them to determine what are the family's values. Counselors are not valueless, she explains. Rather than imposing their values, they state them. And by sharing information, on drugs and alcohol for example, they help the children to develop their own values, and they teach the children coping skills to handle problems they may face. She uses a variety of materials.[27]

These materials and the way she presents them require *involvement* by the children. There are stories to act out, conflict situations to talk about and live into, and role cards in which they play a particular part dealing with anger, in which they "walk in other people's shoes." "They love it!" she said. Through questions that move them into the situation, moral issues become clarified. Ms. Burrows comments, "When they act them out and discuss them, they come to their own conclusions."

For example, in a workshop on racism, based on the life of the Reverend Dr. Martin Luther King, Jr., the children act out the Rosa Parks story, in which she refuses to move to the back of the bus. Another workshop deals with how irrational beliefs ("junk thinking") can cause problems. Ms. Burrows explains that "what you think is how you behave. If you can change the belief system you change behavior." They examine media messages with ten and eleven year olds—what they watch on MTV, TV ads, songs they listen to—helping them to clarify what's being said, what values these messages propose, and how they wish to respond to them.

Since our faith and our beliefs determine how we behave, another way of perceiving the role of church school leaders is as guidance counselors. If children and teachers live into the biblical stories the same way that the school children act out the situations described above, they have a chance of incorporating those eternal values into their belief systems. Those values will become a source for behavior. The development of an aware faith will enable each one to face the exigencies of life from a transcendent perspective. Such a way of learning becomes transformational.

Awakening to Spiritual Awareness and Implications

We are, at our essence, spiritual beings. Having been created in the image of God (Gen. 1:26-27), how could we be anything else? We are not human beings on a spiritual journey, but spiritual beings on a human journey.

Becoming conscious of our spirituality and aware of our continuing need for spiritual enrichment, then, is a necessary part of our developing maturity. Our physical nature is nourished, grows, and matures by the things we eat and the way we use our minds, the things we choose to read and watch on TV, the way we were taught in school, the kind of entertainment we attend. Our spiritual nature is enhanced by our encounter with Scripture; our experiences in worship, and especially in the sacraments; our sensitivity to people and the world around us; and ultimately in our relationship with God, the Ultimate Reality and the Ground of Being, with Jesus, the Christ, and with the presence and action of the Holy Spirit in our lives.

Jesus pointed out that the Realm of God is among/within/in the midst us (see Luke 17:21). Jesus embodied the reality of God's Realm in his being, and Jesus is saying that we are able to embody/incarnate it in ours. Our awareness of that transcendent reality is what is referred to as the Christ consciousness dwelling in us. The extent to which we are able to be aware of the indwelling Christ determines the level of our faith development and the depth of our spiritual life. The presence, activity, and movement of the Holy Spirit in our lives moves us along in our spiritual awareness. How do we develop our innate spirituality and that of our children?

How can we be in touch with the presence of the Holy Spirit in our lives?

Madeline L'Engle tells of being awakened as a very small child and taken by her grandmother out onto the beach to see what must have been an unusually brilliant night sky. "That first sight of the heavens stretched across the ocean and brilliant with stars was," she says, "although I was no way nearly old enough to call it that, my first numinous experience."[28]

Such numinous experiences can continue for children and adults if we open ourselves to the possibilities inherent in ourselves and in the universe. Watching sunsets, listening to great music, holding a newborn baby, listening to a seashell or the wind in the trees, smelling a flower, and sharing an experience of God's presence with another person open the channel to the spiritual world.

Charles L. Whitfield remarks that "spirituality is *experiential*. We cannot know it ultimately through our intellect or through reason. It is not knowable. It is only be-able." Such awareness is crucial in our becoming a whole person and "especially for discovering and ultimately liberating the 'Child Within,' our Real and True Self."[29]

There is within each of us a divine child, that child/person whom God imaged at our creation. In his introduction to *Reclaiming the Inner Child,* Jeremiah Abrams comments that each person begins life with an awareness of the infinite, the other, which we would call God.[30] However, a left-brained educational system tunes that out. Consequently there is also the Wounded Child, a product of our experiences as children. Increasingly books are being written and workshops are being held on helping persons to recovering that inner child.[31] The qualities of childlikeness that Jesus admonished the disciples to emulate have been variously described in many of these books as awe, wonder, joy, sensitivity, openness, spontaneity, lovingkindness, acceptance, playfulness, humor, trust, vulnerability, freedom to grow, aliveness, energy, creativity, and imagination.

Perhaps, in working with children we can find release/healing/forgiveness/transformation for that Wounded Child so that our Divine Child, our true Self, and these childlike qualities can emerge again, as the cartoon on page 35 suggests.

Recapturing Childlike Fun

Another way to recapture that inner child is to allow yourself to be playful. Instead of getting bogged down by the curriculum, be free with it. Be creative. Be yourself. Don't slavishly follow what someone else has created. Then everyone will learn more, there will be a deeper sense of community, and everyone will have fun.

Fun? In church school? Yes, fun! We get so serious about our faith that we lose the joy and excitement. It gets heavy and tedious and boring. Children begin to see God, Jesus, and the Holy Spirit that way, too. But Jesus had a sense of humor that somehow gets lost in translation. We need, again, to become as a little child and experience the joy.

The *Brain/Mind Bulletin* reports on research showing that "learning is more effective when it is fun."[32] In this report, Kline suggests that we are all geniuses, but school hasn't encouraged us to notice what's inside of us. He recommends that parents truly listen to their children. Also he suggests that teachers put learning into new contexts that are not associated with school and are, therefore, more fun. He suggests using music creatively, engaging in fantasy, allowing students to play the role of teacher, and physically acting out abstract ideas. All of these ideas are basic to using TBS successfully.

At an annual meeting of the Association of Presbyterian Church Educators, Glen Bannerman received the Educator of the Year award. He had spent thirty-one years developing and teaching courses in recreation (*re*creation!) at the Presbyterian School of Christian Education in Richmond, Virginia. On receiving the award, he suggested that "we all have a child within us that's trying to be let out." But somehow our society says, "'Quit playing, get serious and mature. Grow Up!' And our children look around and say, 'Grow up to what?' And we look at our adult society and say, 'Is that what we really want our children to grow up to?'"

Consequently we kill our inner child. "We need to think in terms of letting that child out. We need to continue to find ways for that to happen."[33]

A New Emphasis on Spiritual Education

An increasing number of books are being written about education for spiritual growth in children. The Griggs Educational Resources Series offers a number of books by Judy Gattis Smith in which she uses right-brain activities and all the senses to recapture and enhance awe, wonder, joy, imagination, and creativity to the Realm of God's reality and love.[34]

Iris V. Cully's informative and comprehensive book *Education for Spiritual Growth* provides an enormous reference to spiritual development. It includes biblical, historical, theological, and psychological resources, and it draws on the contemplative in both Eastern and Western traditions and discusses faith development from a variety of models. Cully comments:

> Education for spirituality may be hampered by the agenda that frequently form the core of religious education curricula. . . . This attitude is unfortunate. Spiritual models can be incorporated into teaching if the curriculum is designed to permit flexibility and a degree of freedom.[35]

In her chapter "Nurture in Spirituality," she follows the developmental modes of Piaget, Erikson, Kohlberg, and Fowler, describing briefly how teachers of children from nursery age through adolescence can nurture spiritual growth.

While she and others talk about nurturing and sharing faith, the emphasis is still a developmental/educational model. The concept that children have an intuitive sense of the spiritual realm and are able to exercise that knowing in biblical study is simply not recognized. It's not a matter of incorporating spiritual models into the teaching of curricula but assuming a basically spiritual orientation as an approach to biblical study and its application to life.

We are reminded of St. Augustine's prayer: "Eternal God, from whom we come and to whom we return and in whom we live and move and have our being, our hearts are restless until they find their rest in thee." If we know ourselves as coming from God we know God's presence in our lives from the very beginning. That sense needs to be nurtured in very small children and regained for ourselves. In studying the Bible with children, we may in fact find it again.

For example, in I Samuel 3 several nuances stand out. Although Samuel was probably under the age of twelve and God rarely spoke and few people had visions at that particular time, God chose to speak to Eli through Samuel. Notice (v. 9) that Eli was aware (perceived) that God was speaking to Samuel, and he suggested how Samuel might respond. Even though Samuel was afraid (v. 15) to tell Eli of his vision, he did so at Eli's urging. And Eli was also aware that God had spoken to Samuel. Do we in fact trust that God speaks to children, that we might suggest how they might respond, urge them to share their visions and their experiences, and finally assume that God also speaks to us through children?

Eastern religions, such as Hinduism and Buddhism, assume that even little children are in touch with God. The Reverend Roshi Jiju-Kennett, Abbess of the Mt. Shasta Zen abbey in Mt. Shasta, California, who was raised a devout Anglican, writes: "Every small child knows how to meditate properly; it is only after we have 'educated' it that its body and mind become separated."[36] At a training session on Zen Buddhist meditation, in answer to a question about the Anglican faith in which she was raised, she said, "If the Church had taught me how to pray, they never would have lost me!"

Spiritual life and education are much discussed in the field of Transpersonal Psychology. As its name implies, this psychology goes beyond (trans) personal concerns for body, mind, and emotions to include the spiritual. An eminent transpersonal psychologist, Frances Vaughan, comments: "Perhaps if the inner life were not so badly neglected in the educational system, there would be less need for remedial work in psychotherapy in order to redress the balance between inner and outer development."[37]

Vaughan also states: "Children seldom share their inner world of fantasy and perception with adults, because sympathetic, understanding adults are rare." The implication for church school leaders is quite obvious. She comments that educational institutions, and that would include most church schools today, do not deal with intuition but rather close off the inner world "where intuition is nourished, although children and adolescents often have a very active intuition." She goes on to say: "A child whose natural intuitive abilities are strong enough to survive social censure may develop into an exceptionally creative person, but what about all those whose talents simply remain repressed or underdeveloped?"[38]

It is through our creativity that we best express our inner awareness of ourselves as part of God's good creation. It is through intuition that the Holy Spirit speaks to us "in sighs too deep for words." The church school needs to be aware of the need for this spiritual enrichment of the inner life.

In the preface to *The Spiritual Life, Learning East and West,* Westerhoff and Eusden state: "Spirituality has to do with being an integrated person in the fullest sense. . . . We seem to grasp that we are also spiritual beings and that our universe is also comprised of a nonphysical, spiritual dimension which can be known directly by encounter and participation."[39] They comment on the currently increasing search for this spiritual dimension among people throughout the world, of "persons on a journey toward a consciousness in which subjective, depth experiences are as important as objective, empirically measurable, rational explanations."[40] They suggest, in my phraseology, that East is East and West is West and the twain *have* met.

In talking about spiritual awareness and ways of knowing, Westerhoff comments that religion can only be put into metaphorical images, symbolic words, or poetry.

> Religion is better sung than recited, better danced than believed, better painted than talked about. . . . That is why children—those who are dependent, nonrational, nonproductive beings—can have religious experiences and, more importantly, can help adults, who have become independent, rational, and productive, to rediscover the holy.[41]

A caution needs to be raised here. Psychotherapists are uncovering much spiritual abuse. For example, when I was eight years old, a church school teacher informed me that if I did not learn my Bible verses I would go straight to hell. Recently a Roman Catholic who does spiritual direction shared with a group that a little girl, because of her responsiveness in catechetical class and from some interior wisdom, assumed that she would be Mary in the Christmas pageant. When someone else was chosen she was stunned and asked the teacher why. The teacher replied: "Of course you can't be Mary. Mary was blonde, and you're not!" I suspect that such experiences are legion in religious education throughout Christendom.

There is in all children a latent potential for spiritual awareness. Our purpose and task are to bring it out and enhance it and to be very careful not to destroy it. Sue Comstock, in "Nurturing the Spiritual Experience of Children," tells about five-year-old Betsy, who in talking with her church school teacher about prayer said, "Sometimes when I go to bed at night I say the Lord's Prayer that my brother taught me." The teacher responded with, "Oh, that's nice," and went on to explain how Jesus had taught the Lord's prayer to his disciples. Betsy responded with great conviction, "Well, my brother taught me!"

Betsy was coming out of her *experience,* the teacher out of her need to *educate.* Comstock says, "If the teacher had simply stopped with, 'That's nice' or 'That sounds like a special time' or 'Can you tell me more about that?' it is possible the sharing would have continued."[42]

This little incident illustrates a number of matters that are intrinsic to Transforming Bible Study. First of all, recall Madeline L'Engle's admonition, "Don't answer questions children haven't asked." Perhaps Betsy knew that Jesus originally taught that prayer—she'll learn that eventually anyway. Betsy's interest was in talking about her prayer experience, and the teacher needed to listen attentively to the depth of what Betsy was trying to communicate. She needed to listen attentively to what children have to say and use children's interests as a basis for conversation.

In talking about contemplative prayer on a TV program on various religions, an Orthodox priest mentioned the Jesus prayer. The reporter began questioning the priest about the content of that prayer. He replied, "When you pray, don't theologize." Likewise, when you are talking about people's experience with prayer, don't try to teach. As Westerhoff suggests, "teachers must be models of what they desire others to become; they are to be spiritual mentors and not instructors."[43]

The clue to what might have happened is in the question "Can you tell me more about that?" By drawing Betsy out, the teacher might have found out more about Betsy's spiritual experience and even shared her own—that is, the teacher may have lived into the question. The opportunity to talk deeply about a child's faith is a moment not to be lost.

Learning Together

> The concept of teacher as student
>   and student as teacher
>   is not new.
> It has been spoken of by the wise souls
>   of every generation.
> There is much learning
>   to be derived from the teaching process.
> But the teacher must remain the student
>   if the teacher is to grow.[44]

When I lead teacher training workshops, I give a copy of this piece of wisdom to the teachers on a 3-inch by 5-inch card with the suggestion that they place it where they can see it before they begin preparing a church school lesson. It expresses cogently the idea of learning together.

People can't be expected to give what they haven't got. It's understandable that church school leaders come to their task with trepidation. Many "teach" because they have their own children in the church school and have been persuaded by someone, or their own conscience, to be leaders. Perhaps someone has approached an unsuspecting parent with the problem of insufficient leaders and psychologically twisted that parent's arm so that he or she volunteered. With little experience or training, such volunteers often feel overwhelmed by the task. All they are able to do is replicate their childhood experiences in church school.

People who have a degree in education and experience in teaching in public or private schools are often especially sought after as leaders in the church school. While it is true that many have experience in relating to a group of children, they tend to use the methods of the public school system type-two methodology. However, this approach is not effective, as indicated above, in developing faith and spiritual awareness.

The best church school leaders are interested in learning more about the Bible, want to deepen their faith, enjoy being with and respect children and youth, and realize that they can learn from them. It is not necessary to be a trained school teacher. Occasionally a person who seems like a "scared little rabbit" but wants to learn and has some special gift of which she or he is only dimly aware will just blossom as a church school leader—beginning usually by helping out in a classroom with a well-trained leader.

Within this new paradigm, being a leader does not require the routine of unzip heads, pour in knowledge, zip up heads. In one church school the leaders are called "Friends in Learning." It isn't really necessary to know very much to start with. Having grown up in the church people usually have at least a smattering of knowledge about God and Jesus and the Bible and the meaning of faith. Start there. Ask yourself these questions: What is my faith experience, and how would I describe it? What do I already know about God and Jesus and the Bible? Having thought that through a bit, theology emerges: God is, Jesus is, the Bible is, faith is. The next question is vital: How do I *feel* about all this? Confused? Excited? Overwhelmed? Interested? What is most important is sharing that faith, and what you do and don't know, with the children.

Getting Started

The next step is to become aware of what you need to know. How do you find something in the Bible? It has a table of contents. It isn't necessary to be able to recite the names of the books in proper order. I'm not sure I could do that. Simply start using it. But don't try to read it through from start to finish—you'll get bogged down in some very incomprehensible parts. Ask someone for help in how to use it, as a small child who wants to learn would ask someone how to tie a shoe.

There are helpers and helps in every church. Most churches have some basic reference books stashed away some place, or yours may even have a library. The pastor has one too—she or he needed it to get through seminary and uses it for sermon preparation. Again, don't be afraid to ask. Most pastors would be thrilled that there is someone in their congregation who is eager to learn.

Having decided to "teach," don't assume that the curriculum will help anyone to be a good leader. Although some editors and writers are aware of new educational developments, most published curricula are still designed on the old paradigm. Regardless of the reading they may have done in this field, or the workshops they have attended, they still view Christian education as *education* rather than faith development and spiritual awareness. As a curriculum writer, I have found it exceedingly frustrating to try to put new wine into old wineskins.

To begin, simply take the materials given you and

look at the basic structure of the lesson plan;
use the Bible background provided;
try out the suggested creative activities;
watch out for "this is what it means" and "tell the children";
use the ideas in chapter 3 on adapting curricula.

Begin preparing with a childlike prayer: "God, I need help. I don't understand this at all. Enlighten me." Leave a silent, listening space. God can only answer prayers if we listen. Read Scripture. Follow the suggestions in chapter 2. Go into the classroom with the attitude "I'm going to learn more today than they are," knowing that the Holy Spirit will be there guiding each one all the way.

Enjoy!

Chapter 2
Getting the Gospel in Your Gut

Transforming Bible Study

Transforming Bible Study is a double entendre—that is, it can be understood in two ways. It is not only a method for transforming the way Bible study is done, but also a process that becomes a transforming experience. To that I can personally attest. "Getting the gospel in your gut" is my definition. As long as the gospel, and indeed the whole biblical story, remains a "head trip"—only an intellectual exercise—it cannot be transforming. It is only when it becomes a part of your whole being—mind, body, emotions, spirit, and community—that it changes the way you perceive, feel, and respond.

The method incorporates a critical examination of the biblical text and psychological insights unfolded around the text developed at the Guild for Psychological Studies, San Francisco, California. It was adapted, beginning in 1971, by Walter Wink, then Professor of Biblical Interpretation at Union Theological Seminary, New York, and currently at Auburn Theological Seminary, New York. His purpose was to make the method available in a limited way to people struggling to lead Bible study, primarily with adults, in a meaningful way in a variety of settings.

There are three components to the method:

Accessing the text by reading it, looking at the setting and the social situation, and doing whatever literary and historical criticism of the text is necessary for the particular group.
Amplifying the text with "feeling" questions so that we identify with the people in the story.
Applying the text to our lives by using arts and crafts, drama, movement, sharing, and written dialogues.

Wink describes the goal as "so to move among these mighty texts that we are transformed." To be transformed does not mean simply adding to an old structure, but renovating the structure itself. Critically accessing the text frees us from old preconceptions and frees the text to "speak in ways we are accustomed to *not* hearing." Amplifying the text begins to "get the gospel in our gut." Applying the text through exercises enables us to reflect on its meaning for our lives and thus to begin to change. But it is in doing all three steps together that we are driven deeper, "to that lost dimension, that uncharted land, where our own true face is known, and where what God is and what living is are one."[1]

Another way to say this is described by Parker Palmer in *To Know As We Are Known.* In his teaching he encourages his students not only to listen to the teacher and to one another, but also to "the voice of the subject." In order to be obedient to truth, "we must strain to hear what the subject is saying about itself beyond all our interpretations." Instead of just viewing the subject we need to interview it so that it can speak back to us "in ways surprisingly independent of our own preconceptions." It is in listening and paying attention to this "otherness" that "we are drawn out of merely knowing into being known."[2]

Since the Bible, and the Gospel stories of Jesus in particular, is the subject and the truth we wish to hear, we need to read it with great care. Often Bible stories are so familiar to us that we impose what we think we already "know" on them. Rather, we must always read them as though for the first time so that by encountering Jesus we can encounter and know ourselves.

Robert McAfee Brown, in *The Bible Speaks to You* begins his chapter on "The Unexpected Character of the Good News (What Makes Jesus So Important)," with a scroll that states:

BE IT HEREBY ENACTED
that every three years all people
shall forget whatever they have learned
about Jesus, and begin the study all over again * * *[3]

Our most important task, Wink suggests, is to encounter Jesus. He must be our primary interest, "not just his teaching but how he discovered it, lived it, made it the very pattern of his flesh."[4] Who was Jesus before he was understood or described as God incarnate, the source of all healing, the only-begotten Son of God, Messiah? How did he relate to God as "Abba" (Daddy), to the healing

Source? How did he understand forgiveness, the kingdom, the Son of Man? "In short, before Jesus was taken up into the Christian myth, with all the incomparable riches that flowed from that, how did Jesus relate to his own myth: the inner unfolding of his own being?"[5]

"Christianity is not centered around moral teaching, but around a person" comments the contemporary Cistercian priest, monk, and abbot Thomas Keating. The way we meet Jesus in Scripture involves the same dynamic that happens in making friends with anyone. "You have to spend time together, talk together, listen to each other, and get to know each other."[6]

The purpose then is to encounter God, Creator, Word and Holy Spirit, as revealed to us in Jesus.

The method used is a Socratic, dialogical method of asking questions. The process begins with *accessing* the biblical text by reading it. Once the biblical text has been read, it must be studied critically and intelligently. As Wink points out: "The value of the critical method is that it defends the text from our projecting on it our own biases, theologies, and presuppositions." We have to allow the text "to be different from what we want, even to be offensive." This critical analysis is absolutely necessary "if we are interested in being transformed, and not simply confirmed in what we already know."[7]

The focus is the text itself, not our preconceptions around it. The text must stand on its own, unencumbered by our previous understandings, our projections, or our current theology. As suggested before, there are many questions to which there are no "right" answers, even in the critical examination of the biblical text, where scholars often disagree.

This is followed by the process of *amplification,* or experiencing ourselves in the text by living into the Scripture text so that it becomes vivid for us. *"Only as the text comes alive for us can we attempt to hear again the question that occasioned the answer provided by the text."*[8]

As we move into this amplification of the text we must work with it as though for the first time, with a childlike beginner's mind. What we seek here are all the valuable insights people may have around the text. When this is done we allow the Holy Spirit to open our minds and hearts to often surprising new understandings. Since this is done in a group, insight builds on insight, and in some synchronistic[9] and synergistic[10] way the understandings arrived at by the whole group go far beyond anything we could have anticipated or arrived at alone.[11] It provides a hologram of the biblical passage.

Enriched by these new insights, we engage in some personal application of them to our current life. This is probably the most difficult aspect of Wink's method, the one that some people will adamantly resist. Wink explains that we must move beyond understanding the text intellectually or seeing certain parallels with our own lives.

> We need to let it move deeply within us. By music, movement, painting, sculpting, written dialogues, small-group sharing, we can allow the text to unearth that part of our personal and social existence which it calls forth to be healed, forgiven, made new.[12]

Simply understanding a passage intellectually or seeing some relevance to the world in which we live will not transform us. We need to allow the passage to speak to the depths of who we are and whom we can possibly become. To aid us in doing this we use all of those methods Wink describes above. This does not mean that we need to be musicians, dancers, artists, or authors. Rather, we need to be ourselves, expressing from our deepest self what the process has revealed to us about ourselves. Through this complete process, transformation can take place.

This is but a brief description of the process of Transforming Bible Study to provide enough background for understanding the process. A thorough explication and description of how to use this method, as I suggested in the preface, is described in Wink's book *Transforming Bible Study*. The method is best learned by attending a workshop with the Winks. June Keener-Wink leads wonderful movement and arts and crafts segments for amplification of the text and its application to our lives.

Using the Method with Children

This method is not another new technique for using the Bible with children. A number of books have been written that explicate creative ways of doing that.[13] However, using TBS with children requires a whole new paradigm, through which "we pass from 'knowing about' reality, to *knowing* it." It means living the questions together through many answers until they become right for us. That requires "new presuppositions, new values, new methods, new beliefs, a new view of knowledge, a person being made new."[14]

The emphasis then is on studying the scripture and sharing our faith *with* the students. Our first task is to discover "what Scripture has to say in its own right." Since, as Wink suggests, the biblical territory is largely unknown, an "unexplored wilderness, of which even the leader is largely ignorant," Bible study requires "the concerted efforts of the entire group."[15] Consequently, this method basically respects everyone's ability, *including the child's,* to access, to amplify, and to apply biblical texts. It also affirms children's ability to think for themselves. Perhaps especially here "a little child shall lead them" (Isa. 11:6).

Additionally Jesus' statements to the disciples concerning the necessity of becoming as a little child in order to access God's Realm (Matt. 18:3; 19:13-15; Mark 10:13-16; Luke 18:15-17) and being humble like a child in order receive Jesus and God into their lives (Matt. 18:5; Mark 9:33-37), suggest that children have an innate affinity for God and for the gospel that somehow adults no longer have. Therefore, what children have to say about the meaning of Scripture, especially for their lives, may be far superior to anything leaders can tell them. It also implies that adults can well learn from children.

It is indeed difficult for leaders to give up control over a learning situation. But Wink points out that the purpose of TBS is "the transformation of persons toward the divine possibilities inherent in them," including and first of all the leader. It is not a technique to make someone a better "teacher." He suggests that until we have had the experience time and again "that others with less training or intelligence have anything to teach us," we will find it difficult to believe that we can "be ministered to by them and educated as to the meaning of these texts for our own lives."[16] That is particularly true of leaders of children.

Many Christian educators will insist that this method cannot be done with children, that it is not age appropriate (especially with children as young as five or six), that children cannot answer questions to which they haven't previously been given the answer. But this objection does not reflect enough respect for the abilities of children to encounter the meaning of a biblical text and its implication for their lives. For over ten years this method of Bible study has worked successfully with church school, vacation church school, and after-school classes of four to twenty children, aged five to fourteen.

Young children work well in small groupings of four, but a small group may be intimidating to older children. This type of Bible study works best in a class of eight to ten children, in which a rapport has developed. The critical biblical study can be done with groups of up to twenty children with a skilled leader. But the amplification and application may need to be done in smaller groups with people skilled in drama, movement, or arts and crafts.

The first step, of course, is your own preparation. The Bible version you choose for the text is critical. Although everyone has her or his own preference, my preference is the New Revised Standard Version. Also, *Gospel Parallels,* a synopsis of the first three Gospels, edited by Burton H. Throckmorton, Jr., is an invaluable tool for a leader.[17] It has Matthew, Mark, and Luke side-by-side with footnotes for similar readings in John, Acts, and the Epistles, and in some of the gnostic gospels, such as the Gospel of Thomas.[18]

In a church school situation with a prescribed curriculum you simply use this method with the Bible passage set for that lesson. Begin by reading the scripture and asking all the who/what/where/why/when/how questions you can manage. What is the setting? Where is the story taking place? Who is involved? What do you know about them? Why are they responding this way? How would you have responded? Why do you suppose they said what they did? What do you suppose they meant? What would you have said? Why?

Then read any biblical background provided in the curricula. *Do not do that the other way around.* Otherwise your own creativity will be limited by what someone else has said about the passage. You may be able to use the suggested activities for amplification and application if they are appropriate, or you may adapt them as necessary.

You need to start your first session with your class by explaining the TBS method in a simple fashion. Children, unfortunately, are so conditioned by being told what to think and how to behave and to giving "right" answers that this process is initially difficult for them. It is important to explain that you will be asking many questions that most of the time don't have "right" answers. The only exception to this is when you have asked someone to look up some information. Then, of course, you will expect an accurate answer.

Most of the time the questions will be wondering and feeling questions, like "I wonder how Jesus felt when . . . "; "I wonder how the disciples, or some other person felt when . . . "; "I wonder why Jesus, or someone else said. . . . " It is also reassuring to look directly at the child or youth and acknowledge an answer with "thank you."

In working this way with children, I often make the statement that God gave us two ears so that what goes in one can come out the other. Only when information comes in our eyes or ears and we express it in some way through our mouths or through an action does it become ours. I also suggest that they not raise their hands to answer the questions but simply share what comes into their minds. That makes the class more informal and relaxed and less like school.

It is usually useful to begin a class period with a song, preferably one that has accompanying actions, that is either a gathering song (call to worship) or has some relation to the theme of the unit. This is a way of helping the children to leave behind what they have come from and of centering them in where they are and what they are about to do.

Then gather in a circle. Tables are for hiding behind and kicking beneath. Tables separate, while circles create closeness, and they make it possible for everyone to see and to hear one another. Additionally, as Wink suggests, they are symbolic: "The circle is a profound image of wholeness, of organic unity, of safety."[19]

Once a routine is established, the children will automatically get their Bibles and sit down. Even first-graders who are just beginning to read can use the Bible. In a small class of four children, aged six through ten, one girl could only read "God" and "and" when the class began in the fall, but by April she could find the passage as fast as anyone and was able to read remarkably well.

When working with children it is best for everyone to have the same translation, or the children will have difficulty following along in reading and will be confused by the different renderings. Even here I still prefer the New Revised Standard Version because it's important to learn the traditional biblical language and to use the best text possible. If the Bible is never heard and never used in the church school, then it is never understood when it is read at worship, and it always sounds strange. If your church normally uses another Bible translation, try to be consistent and use it to reinforce patterns of language. Do avoid using modern paraphrases of the biblical text, such as the Living Bible, because the interpretations involved will prejudice the children's ability to think for themselves. The best translations, such as the New Revised Standard Version, the New English Bible, and the Jerusalem Bible, make a more literal attempt to reproduce the grammar and syntax of the biblical language.

Begin the process by reading the text. There are a number of ways to do this. My preference is to read it as a drama, which it largely is. Ask for volunteers to read the parts of the narrator and the various people involved in the dialogue, and ask everyone to read group parts, or divide them up among various people. Thus who is talking to whom is much clearer when the text says, "And he said." There are two cautions here: Never assign someone to read, even if you think you know the child or youth, because you can never be sure who has a reading problem or an emotional problem that would make reading that particular text at that particular time difficult. For the same reason, don't go around the circle with each person reading a verse. That chops up the scripture too much, and most children won't follow or listen to what is read, but will be figuring out which verse they will have to read. If there is no dialogue, and if the section is long, it can be appropriate to have each paragraph read by a different person, but again on a volunteer basis. Also, don't always rely on "the best reader in the class." Help the children to struggle with the text, reading the difficult place names and other words yourself. If a slow reader volunteers, ask that child whether he or she would like for you to read, too. Somehow slow readers generally think that's a big deal and enjoy doing it.

When the Scripture is a Psalm, have it read antiphonally—one part of the verse by one group, the other corresponding section by another group, as Hebrew poetry is written—not verse by verse. For example:

1. The Lord is my shepherd,
2. I shall not want.
1. He makes me lie down in green pastures;
2. He leads me beside still waters.

Some passages may be read by everyone together, such as the Magnificat.

Once the Scripture has been read and you are faced with the critical process you may assume that children can't understand it and couldn't care less. Wrong! They are fascinated by where that unpronounceable town is and what it looked like and why people behaved the way they did and what they wore and how they traveled. Remind them that the biblical places really exist today. It's not Oz. Use maps; all those old teaching pictures that are stored away somewhere; and current pictures and articles on Israel, Jordan, Syria, the Left Bank, and Palestinian refugees that are in your newspapers and magazines. If some of these places were in the previous night's TV or radio news, mention that. Sometimes it is also possible to build on the social studies the children are doing in school.

Also a knowledge of the biblical languages, Hebrew and Greek, is helpful here. Obviously not many church school leaders will know these languages—nor do all clergy. Nevertheless your pastor would probably be delighted to help with biblical criticism. This is also an excellent way to involve the pastor in the Christian education program. A monthly meeting of the church school staff, led by the pastor or the Christian education director can be invaluable in providing some background on the social and political setting of the text and the context within the particular book being studied. There may also be other knowledgeable laypeople who have lived or traveled extensively in the Holy Land who could share pictures and experiences of being in the places mentioned in the text.

Often good church school curricula will provide appropriate background in the material for leaders. This is one basis on which to evaluate the curriculum being used. Does it give historical background, provide some critical discussion of the text, or does it give predigested statements of what it means?

Older church school students may find some of this material in Bible dictionaries, atlases, brief commentaries, or curricula resource books when the students arrive, and they can provide it at appropriate times as the leader goes through the text.

When the scripture has been read and the setting and background understood one of the best ways to get into the text is to act it out. It is not necessary for those doing the acting to remember exactly what the text says. In fact, it's better to let the children, and especially youth, use their own words—even slang—as that literally allows them to get into it. What children say and how they say it reveals much about their perceptions around the text, which may need some discussion and emendations. In a small class and with younger children it is often useful for the leader to take a part to help move the action or dialogue along.

It can also be useful for each child to mime each of the characters and discuss how they felt being each of them. This miming is particularly useful in those too well-known stories from the Hebrew Scriptures, some of the Gospel stories, and Jesus' parables, such as the Samaritan, where listeners often think they know what's going on until they have to "feel-into" a familiar character.

Creating Questions

Once the story is clear in each child's mind, the leader begins by asking questions. In preparing for a session, begin with the first verse of the passage and write down all the questions you can think of about that verse and each succeeding verse. Before you can lead in this way you have to make the passage your own. You must live into it beyond the purely rational; experience it yourself and see where it specifically applies to your life. You constantly have to ask yourself, "In what way am I like that person?" and "How does that apply to me?" But remember that the insights gained are yours. Although they may determine the direction in which you perceive the passage to be moving, the children and youth may have different perceptions from which you will learn and may force you to shift gears as you lead.

As an example, let's take the story of the Samaritan (Luke 10:30-37), probably the best-known New Testament story. For the sake of simplicity here, we'll ignore the question that elicited the parable, and a discussion of what a parable is. That should be done in a church school class if there is sufficient time, especially with the older children and youth. The following questions elicit the full range of possibilities within the text. They would need to be modified for time restrictions and for the children's abilities to understand, but resist the impulse to make it too simple.

Verse 30. Who might the "man" have been? Where was he going? Why had he been in Jerusalem? Where is Jerusalem? What is the altitude? Where is Jericho? Altitude? How far is Jerusalem from Jericho? What's the terrain like? (Use an atlas and pictures.) What happened to the man? Was that unusual for the place? What were the robbers after? What condition was he in when they left? Given the setting, how long might he live?

Verse 31. What is a priest? Where was he going? Why? Why did he pass by? What might have happened had he stopped? If the man died what would happen to the priest? (See Lev. 21:1-3, 11.)

Verse 32. What is a Levite? Where was he going? Why? Why did he pass by?

Verse 33. What is a Samaritan? What was the relationship between Samaritans and Jews? What might he have been doing in Jerusalem? In Jericho?

Verse 34. What did the Samaritan do for the injured man? What did the Samaritan use to bind up the injured man's wounds? Why did the Samaritan pour oil and wine on the man? What do oil and wine each do? What kind of a beast was he riding? How far was the inn from where the man was hurt? What might the innkeeper say to the Samaritan's request? How might the Samaritan have taken care of the wounded man?

Verse 35. What would a denarii pay for? In net worth, what did the Samaritan give the innkeeper? What about his promise? Would the innkeeper trust the Samaritan? When would he come back? How was the innkeeper sure?

With *verse 36* we return to the context. Notice how Jesus phrases the question he asks. Ask it. What does the scribe say? What doesn't he say? How does that relate to the question in verse 29, which precipitated the parable, and the original question in verse 25?

Having gotten the sense of the parable and the context and

extended meaning from the questions, you now get to the essence of the story: Why did the Samaritan stop? What do we do to this passage when we call him the *good* Samaritan?

The examples below will give you some sense of the experiences that children bring to this parable. In using this questioning method it is important to acknowledge the insights the children and youth share. One good way is simply to say "thank you." But also be aware of those children who feel unacknowledged and may need extra attention. Then ask the question again and again, pushing the awareness deeper and deeper to overcome their natural resistance to facing the reality within themselves.

It is also important not to let older children and youth get into a debate on their insights into and interpretations of the passage. These students may come from different religious backgrounds, and each person's insight is a result of his or her experiences in life and with the particular passage. It is, therefore, inappropriate for you to declare a student's response "wrong." We need to allow space for disagreement in interpretation, to be gracious enough to acknowledge that there is no right answer, that we each bring valuable insights to the story or passage.

Occasionally discussions around the implications and application of this text descend into an argument on whether or not to pick up hitchhikers. If someone raises the issue, simply ask, "Would you? Have you ever? Why? What is your experience?" But don't let the matter evolve into an argument about the problems involved. Push for the deeper reasons that elicit an understanding of compassion.

In leading younger children through the text the kind of questions that work best are "I wonder why . . ?"; "I wonder what he meant when he said . . ?"; "Why do you suppose . . ?"; "How do you suppose she felt when . . ? "; "How would you have felt if. . . ?"

Keeping Things on Track

Intuition and insights come rapidly for children. They often get excited, bounce around, wave their hands, and say, "Oh. . . . Oh!" They also have a difficult time verbalizing these often somewhat intangible insights. Unfortunately, too, not everyone can talk at once, and the insights get lost, but often will come again. In a small group of four children, ages six through ten, one child was very excited and wanted to share an insight that had occurred to her, but I was unable to get to her at the moment. When I did ask her for her insight, she said, "It went out the other ear."

It is sometimes possible for younger children to write down one or two words that will help in remembering the intuitive insight. Urge them to do that. But sometimes ideas and insights are so ephemeral that they simply disappear. However, they have a way of reemerging as the process progresses. When older children encounter this problem suggest that they write their insights down before trying to verbalize them, giving them a chance to solidify from the often abstract insight that comes through intuition. The value of doing this for myself comes from having had the experience of perceiving totally nonrationally some perceptive understanding around a passage and the deep sense that it was not I speaking, but the Holy Spirit speaking through me.

Sometimes children respond with "smart-aleck" answers. The initial, gut reaction of most leaders is to cringe, put-down, remonstrate, lecture, or ignore such remarks—but often in such comments is gold! When followed up with an appreciative question (such as "That's an interesting response. Can you say more about what you mean?"), all kinds of possibilities are opened. But that takes patience and an awareness of who the child is. If the child is really trying to get attention—even adverse attention—or is being disruptive, a simple question as to why he or she made such a remark will usually make that child back off. If you suspect that there may be something special in the remark, ask the question in another way and see what happens. Or simply ask the child to explain in another way what he or she meant. (For examples, see follow-up questions on pp. 63 and 66.)

Having been encountered by new insights and perhaps by the movement of the Holy Spirit it is time to make this a part of ourselves, to see its *application*. This is where leaders will often back off because of group resistance, but it is absolutely essential if the text is to be relevant to people's lives. It is an extension of the insightful/intuitive awareness that was begun in the amplification process. Up until now, most of the work has been intellectual and left-brained—the thinking side. If it is left there, it remains an intellectual, irrelevant exercise. Now it is time to engage the right-brain—the emotional, reflective side.

Using again the Samaritan parable, ask the question "Where are you wounded/hurting?" to address the application of this parable to the personal lives of the children or youth. It is in identifying with the injured man for whom the Samaritan stopped that we get in touch with our woundedness and thus learn compassion. As Henri Nouwen suggests in *The Wounded Healer,* it is through compassion that we recognize that the need we feel for love also resides in other people and that the cruelty we see in the world "is also rooted in our own impulses. When they kill, we know that we could have done it; when they give life, we know that we can do the same."[20]

The exercise that specifically moves us into an encounter with our woundedness is to draw, to paint, to sculpt, or to move/dance into that part of us which is wounded and hurting. This sounds abstract because there is no way we can access our woundedness intellectually. You cannot "think the right answer." The only meaningful answer comes from the depths of our being as we allow it to move through our deepest Selves and out into some physical expression. It is absolutely necessary that the leader and any helpers participate in this activity. It gives credibility to what the children are doing. Also it is inhibiting for a leader or a helper to walk around the room, observing and commenting on what the children or youth are doing.

One very affective way of working with this on your own or with children and youth is to take a piece of clay and let your hands intuitively mold what comes from your unconscious. When you begin you may have absolutely no idea of what your wounded part is. If, like me, your artistic level is that of a five-year-old you may well feel totally intimidated. Simply hold the clay in your hands, shut your eyes, and sit with it for a moment or two. As the clay warms up, let your hands work with it. After a while, open your eyes and see what your unconscious has created. What does it look like? What part of you or your experience does it represent? A leader needs to allow at least ten minutes for this process to reveal some inner woundedness.

Having done this literally dozens of times, my experience is that each time something new emerges. Sometimes it's a huge struggle. Other times awareness of what that current wound is comes in the amplification process through some insight I have written down. But no matter how many times I do this it's always revealing, healing, and transforming.

When you choose application activities from either the curriculum or from those you have devised, it is important to make sure the action leads the children and youth into their own self-expression. Many church school craft activities are simply cut-and-paste busy work. Clay, paint, and craypas, or crayons used to create abstractions are best. Never force children to explain what they mean, but do invite them to share if they wish.

In working with youth aged eleven through eighteen, it is useful to get them to struggle with the question, "What do we do to this story when we call it 'The *Good* Samaritan'?" That provides an opportunity to lead into a discussion of values clarification and the problem of works righteousness vs. grace, of earning salvation rather than responding to it. Then follow the discussion up with a similar dramatic situation that they face in school or at home in which they act out various solutions.

After the drama or drawing and sharing, you might want to sing a quiet song, listen to some quiet music, or go for a quiet walk. Then end the class with a prayer of thanksgiving and benediction that emerges from the process.

Examples

Here are some examples of how TBS will work in a variety of circumstances with children and youth.

At a large downtown church, I sat in on a class of children aged five through eight at the request of the leader. With no preconceived idea of what would happen, my only commitment was to be true to the text (the parable of the Samaritan) and to see what these young children might do with it. Having worked with this passage a number of times, I was very familiar with the background and the story. It would have been useful to have had an atlas to show what the road from Jerusalem to Jericho looks like still today. However, my concern that morning was simply to have them live into the story.

The regular class leader began by reading the story from the Bible, then had the children tell it back to her using the flannelgraph. My first suggestion was that we act out the story. The class was small in number, and they lacked someone to play the innkeeper; so I took that part. The students ran through the story hurriedly and without much consciousness or direction. It would have been better if we had begun by narrating the story: "A man was going down from Jerusalem to Jericho—and what happened?" Without urging, the children will act out the answer by pretending to beat up on the "man." Then ask "stage-directing" questions:

L: What condition is he in now? Who came next? Do you think he was walking? Or riding? On what? How did you feel when you rode by? How do you think the injured man felt? (*Repeat for the Levite.*) What did the Samaritan do? How do you suppose the injured man felt then? What happened next?

These questions would have involved the children more deeply and perhaps elicited a better response when I began asking questions. Learn from experience! However, following is the conversation that did take place while I was playing the innkeeper.

L: Wow! Your friend's in pretty bad shape. What happened to him?

S: He got beat up by robbers.

L: You're not going to bring him in here, are you?

S: Yes. I'm going to take care of him. And when I leave tomorrow, I'll pay you to take care of him.

L: Look, this is a motel, not a long-term care facility. How do I know you'll leave enough money? He might be here for months in that condition.

S: Here's my charge card.

L: (*I had a hard time not laughing!*) Well, I guess that will do.

Complimenting them on how well they had done, I had the children gather around the table. They informed me that their leader had said they could draw a picture, but she had given no suggestions as to what to draw. For no apparent reason they all began to draw a house.

In order to find out how much the children understood about what we had just done, my questioning went like this:

L: Why do you think the Samaritan stopped?

S: (*almost in chorus*) I haven't the slightest idea!

L: Let's give that some thought. Don't you have any ideas?
S: Nope. (*Silence, except for some arguments about the use of crayons.*)

They continued to work on their pictures while we talked—about ten to fifteen minutes. From this experience, I learned that this is a great way to have a discussion with young children. But you have to be prepared for interruptions and be willing to repeat your questions as often as necessary. In a case like this it's helpful to start by talking about similar experiences they may have had.

L: What would you do if you found someone hurt?
S: Call the police. (*A girl reminded me of the time her father found a man lying in the church parking lot after worship and used the phone in my office to call the police.*)
L: What else can you do? What about the hurt person? (*They were each adamant that you should do nothing other than call the police, that you have to be very careful because you might get hurt helping someone. The childhood realities of living in a city!*) Suppose the person hurt is a friend on your block who fell off her bike in front of the house you're drawing?
S: Go call Mommy (*or Daddy*). Have her (*or him*) call the ambulance.
L: When you fall and scrape your knee, which helps most, the bandages or Mommy's kisses?
S: The kisses. (*A boy insisted that it could also be Daddy's kisses, and I wholeheartedly agreed. A girl whose father was a doctor insisted that the bandages had to come first and were very important!*)
L: So what might you do for a hurt friend?
S: Be with him.
S2: Try to comfort her. Loan her my "blankie."
L: Could you draw a friend who has been hurt? Why do you suppose the Samaritan stopped?

There was another interruption about the use of crayons. I just waited for them to work it out. My sense now is that they were using this space to work through my question. I asked again:

L: Why do you suppose the Samaritan stopped?
S: (*a boy who had just turned six*) Because he knew what it was like to be hurt.

L: (*I left a silent space*) Could you draw yourself in the picture?
Who would you be?

By this time the students had drawn an ambulance coming to help
their friend, whom they were comforting. We entitled the pictures
"The Samaritan, the Ambulance, and Me," and we hung them up
around the room. I have been quoting that six-year-old boy's
answer ever since.

That same fall, a Korean congregation that met in the same
church building at 2:00 P.M., asked me to lead their church school.
There were about twelve to fifteen children, aged four to fifteen.
Their parents and the pastor and his wife spoke little English, but
the children were quite Americanized from going to school. As
usual we sat in a circle with our Bibles. Those who could barely
read were helped by the older ones. One girl who was four sat on
my lap.

We went through the usual routine of asking questions to get at
the setting and the story, miming each of the characters, talking
about how we felt being each of them, then acting the whole story
out. When we got to the application questions I asked, "Who for
you is the Samaritan?" Silence. My suggestion was, "a North
Korean?" They shuddered! "You don't like that, do you?" More
silence. It made a profound impact.

Asking them to draw themselves in the story—"Where are you
hurting?"—created some problems. They wanted to know whether
they were supposed to draw a picture of the story. My explanation
that they were to draw a picture of a time they had been hurt still
elicited puzzled looks. Most of them drew a picture of the story.
However, a creative thirteen-year-old drew a wonderful three-
frame cartoon of someone's getting hurt, the arrival of an
ambulance, and his being part of the rescue crew—would that I had
made a copy! The little girl who had sat on my lap drew two long
squiggly lines, one red, one brown, with large red and brown blobs
close together. She explained that the red one was "me being hurt"
and the brown one was "someone coming to help." Remember that
she was four years old!

By contrast, when I worked on this parable with a group of
clergy, I got no answer to my question "Why did the Samaritan
stop?" We went round and round with "Because, as the text says,

compassionate," but no understanding could be elicited as to how he might have gotten that way.

Their initial response to the question of what we do to the story when we call him the "good" Samaritan resulted in more silence. Then a tall black man drew himself up haughtily and said sarcastically, "He was a credit to his race." Everyone laughed, and the point was elegantly made!

I first used this method in 1977 when I led a class of eight to ten youths, aged twelve to fourteen, almost equally divided by gender in a small-town church. A number of the class members were the younger siblings of the class I had taught the previous year. Often in families with two or more children, the younger, or especially the middle, child will be rebellious. That was particularly true here and made for challenging and interesting classes.

The general theme for the year was "The Family," and the beginning unit was "The First Families." We emphasized the relationships of the biblical characters with one another and with God. The first lesson, of course, was on the first family, Adam and Eve.

Toward the end of the session about the Garden of Eden story this is what happened:

L: How do we "get back to Eden"? Of course, we can't really. We can never go back, only forward. So here we have this chasm between God and us. (*I drew two parallel lines down the center of a newsprint page, writing* God *on one side and* Us *on the other.*) How do we get across that chasm?

S: Build a bridge.

L: (*I "built a bridge across the chasm" and, of course, it made a cross.*) So how do you get across that bridge?

S: You take a bus.

L: Which bus? (*I drew a bunch of little boxes at the bottom.*) Here are all these buses, like those in the schoolyard. How do you know which one to take? What's it marked?

S: Jesus Christ.

L: So how do you get back into relationship with God?

S: You take a bus, Jesus Christ, across the cross. (*Several class members gave this or a similar answer, almost simultaneously.*)

We ended the session by making representations of this understanding, and hung them up around the room. The pastor was moved by my recounting of the class session and by the craft work.

However, one student's mother, a "traditional" church school leader, on learning about the incident heard only smart-aleck remarks. She could not hear the meaning or relevance behind it. The issue here is that the students were using their own images and metaphors, some of which may be anathema to adults, as they learn to express themselves theologically.

The third lesson that year was the Cain and Abel story (Gen. 4:1-9). In this particular lesson the emphases were on the relationship between Cain and Abel and the enigma of God's rejection of Cain's offering.

L: Would someone please read Genesis 4:1-9. (*Someone did. It would have been better had we read it together as a drama.*) What difference do you notice in the description of Cain's and Abel's offerings in verses 3 and 4? Why do you suppose that might have been? What would that have to do with Abel's offering being accepted by God and Cain's not? What was Cain's response when his offering was not accepted? What does God's question in verses 6 and 7 have to do with it?

The young people were having trouble with these questions. After reading them through later, it was obvious that these questions were not specific and simple enough to get started. There was not enough setting of the scene, especially around verse 1. It would have been better if I had asked who the elder son was. For verse two, I needed to have asked what each had done. It takes practice! We learn from our mistakes and from the children. By switching gears, which was not part of my lesson plan, my questioning focused on a somewhat parallel situation that each person had probably encountered.

L: Did you ever have to go to a birthday party you didn't want to go to?
S: Oh, yeah!
S: Ugh! (*And other similar responses.*)

In order to bring to their consciousness again how they felt about it, they shared their ideas, thoughts, and insights around that for several minutes.

L: Let's pretend it's Martha's birthday and we've all been invited to her party. (*The boys groaned. There were a few strains of "Happy birthday to you."*)

S: No way!

L: Unfortunately, your mother has insisted that you go to the party. What are you going to give Martha?

S: I don't know! (*It was quite obvious that he couldn't care less!*)

L: How about a Barbie doll? (*I handed him my eyeglass case to represent the doll.*) Now we'll all gather over here as though the party were going on. You go out into the hall, then come in and give the present to Martha. (*Predictably, the girls and I gathered around Martha and pretended to look at her presents. The boys stood awkwardly by in a cluster. The boy walked hesitantly into the room and approached Martha.*)

S: Here! (*He shoved the present at her and then turned away. I waited a few minutes to let the behavior sink in.*)

L: Now let's get in our circle again and look at Cain and Abel. What did Cain do for a living?

S: A tiller of the ground.

S: A farmer.

L: What did Abel do?

S: He was a keeper of the sheep

S: A shepherd. (*People around our area did both of these things, and most everyone had a garden.*)

L: I don't know about you, but we didn't have very good gardening conditions last summer—not enough rain. Our beans were tough! But maybe that's good weather for sheep. What might have been the situation with Abel? With Cain? Let's look again at verses 3 and 4. We've just said Abel had a good year, lots of lambs, nice fat sheep. Who will be Abel, deciding to make an offering to God?

S: I will. (*He got up and went to one end of the room.*) Wow, I sure have had a good year. Guess I'd like to make an offering to God to thank him for all the good luck. Here's a nice fat lamb. (*He pretended to scoop one up and went bouncing and singing with the lamb under his arm.*)

L: Thanks for doing that. How about Cain?

S: Maybe he didn't feel so good about his crops.

L: How might he have felt if he had seen Abel come bouncing in from the field to make an offering to God?

S: Like maybe he ought to make one too?

L: Who'd like to act that out?

S: I will. (*This was a girl—no stereotype casting here!*) Wow. I sure didn't have a good year. But that dumb lucky brother of mine made an offering to God, so I suppose I'd better. (*She picked up something from the ground and sulked off with it.*)

L: So what might Cain have given?

S: Rotten pumpkins.

With no preconceptions about how this would go or what the answer might be, that answer was startling. Here again in a smart-aleck remark was golden insight, for that was an incredible theological perception.

L: So how was Cain feeling?

ALL: Angry. Guilty. Mad. Depressed. Jealous. Frustrated.

L: Why?

S: He had to make an offering he didn't really want to make.

S: He was feeling guilty because he didn't want to.

S: He was feeling frustrated because he'd had a lousy year.

S: He was jealous of Abel because he'd had a good year. (*Nearly everyone said something like this, and all of the responses were insightful.*)

L: Then what was Cain's response to the way he was feeling?

ALL: He killed his brother. (*Almost everyone said this together.*)

L: (*I left a silent space to let this sink in.*) Remember that I've said before that our feelings just are what they are; they're our internal response to what's happening, and we don't have any control over our feelings. But we are responsible for our actions as a response to those feelings. Let's look again at verses 6 and 7. What is God saying to Cain? What does God mean by doing well or not doing well? Doing *what* well or not well?

S: Doing the best you can with a bad situation?

S: Something about our response to God?

S: Not being envious of what others have or do?

L: What's the sin couching at the door? Why must he "master" it?

S: His anger.

S: His envy.

S: Wishing he had what Abel had.

S: If he doesn't master it, it will master him.

L: Have you ever felt this way? This angry with a brother or sister or friend? Or with your parents? Can we draw, paint, or make a collage of our feelings?

There was a quiet intensity as we worked on our expressions of our feelings and awareness. Some were able to share these in our prayer circle; others were not. We ended with the affirmation that God accepts and understands our feelings and, when we ask, forgives us for the feelings we are not proud of.

Just prior to writing this book I taught an after-school program for a small-town church. During Advent we were doing the stories in Luke 1. We had done the story of Gabriel's visit to Mary the week before. We began this session with Mary's going to visit Elizabeth, reading it as a play/dialogue and acting it out. Two of the children in the program were Roman Catholic so we spent some time putting Luke 1:28 and 42 together—it took some doing before they realized it was the Hail Mary.

Since only girls were present that week, we read the Magnificat together. The questioning went this way:

L: What do you suppose Mary meant by "My soul magnifies the Lord"? How could her soul magnify God?

S: (*All of a sudden a seven-year-old girl got very excited.*) Magnify . . . magnify . . . like in magnifying glass! Makes it bigger! So you can see it better!

L: What could she see better? (*I asked in awe.*)

S: What this baby would mean to her. What, what, what . . . God meant to her. What, what, what . . . this baby would mean for the world.

We went on to see that the rest of the Magnificat says precisely that. The depth of awareness about the gospel message that becomes available even to young children when this method is used, so that they "get the gospel in their guts," always amazes me and reminds me again that "unless you become as a little child. . . . "

How-to Preparation

To put this method simply, prepare to lead in this manner by following these steps:

- Read the scripture slowly, carefully, prayerfully.
- Write down all the questions you can think of for each verse.
- Ask what the scripture is saying to your life. What is it you personally need to hear? Write this down or record it in your journal and work on it a bit.
- Decide how you are going to have the scripture read.
- Given the group you are going to lead, which of the questions you have asked yourself do you want to use? After working on it for a time, are there others you need to ask? Do you need to do background research to help with the understanding of the setting? Are there other people who might supply this information?
- Redo the questions to fit your situation.
- Are you going to have it acted out? What feeling questions will you ask?
- What other questions do you need to ask to get into the scripture more deeply?
- Decide whether you will have the class draw or use clay or dance/move or write a dialogue or whatever to get into the meaning for their lives. Choose questions to facilitate this.
- Plan some way of their sharing their insights based on time, age, and the size of group and setting.
- Work this whole process through and figure out how much time you will need for each segment. Will that work? Revise.
- Prepare a phrase or two for the closing prayer circle.

Go in peace.

Chapter 3
"If Only We Had . . ."

It really doesn't work very well to say you are committed to using Transforming Bible Study (TBS) in your Christian education program unless you are also willing to do something about the setting in which it occurs. A new paradigm for Christian education warrants a whole new perspective not only on your attitude toward the children and youth and, therefore, on the way you teach but also on the way you arrange and use the room.

All churches have space problems. There is no such thing as a "perfect" Christian education setting. So take the "if onlys" and find creative ways to make them happen. Never be limited by what you currently have. Faith is believing in the unlimited possibilities in yourself, in the situation, and in God.

Adapting Curricula

If only we had a curriculum that fit our church! I have heard that lament numerous times. It's a wonderful wish. Curricula are usually designed for the "average church," which, of course, doesn't exist. Each church, as with each individual, is unique and different.

Curricula are written by Christian educators for specific denominations—such as Southern Baptist, Episcopal, Lutheran and United Methodist—or for groups of denominations—such as the Presbyterian and Reformed Educational Ministries (PREM) and Joint Educational Development's Christian Education, Shared Approaches (JED:CESA). Many churches, usually the more conservative ones, use commercially prepared curricula—such as those published by David C. Cook, Gospel Light, and Standard. There are also some small, independent publishers with a particular orientation—such as Creative Curriculum, published in Maine, and Centerpoint. Each has its own theological and biblical perspective and particular way of teaching a lesson. The task, therefore, is to adapt whatever curriculum you use to the needs of your church.

The process begins when you decide to choose a curriculum. That choice should never be left up to one or two people, regardless of how small your church is. It's wonderful if your church has developed a philosophy of Christian education that has been adopted by your Christian education committee. That may sound like "big church stuff," but a church of any size can develop such a statement by getting together parents, leaders, pastor, and some members of whatever official governing board your church may have to decide:

This is our basic theology.
This is our view of the Bible.
This is our understanding of Christ and the Church.
This is what we want our children to know about the Christian faith.
This is the process we want our children to go through in a Christian education program to develop their faith and be spiritually enriched.
These are our guidelines for choosing a curriculum.

Once that is accomplished you can ascertain what curriculum most closely meets these criteria. Having decided on and purchased a curriculum, you need to get all the leaders and helpers together—that can be two or three people in a small church or whole departments in a larger one. Leaders should each have a copy of their particular age-level curriculum beforehand so they can look it over. When everyone gets together people can ask questions, raise problems, make suggestions for adaptation, and share insights and resources.

Since the Bible contains the basis of our faith, that is where you start any evaluation. Notice how the Bible is used and how the biblical background is presented. If the curriculum simply says, "This passage means thus and so" or "Tell the children . . . " view it with a very skeptical eye. Go through the scripture yourself, asking the questions suggested in chapter 2. If you need more biblical background, use the atlases, Bible dictionaries, and Bible commentaries in your church library, or ask your pastor or Christian education director for help.

Most curricula come with Bible storybooks and leaflets of some sort. These are grave temptations! It's so easy simply to read the story and give the leaflets to the children. This cuts down on preparation time and "gives me something to do." While not all leaders will use Transforming Bible Study, these books and resources stifle a child's and a leader's creativity by doing too much interpretation before their imaginations are released in God's Spirit.

Some Bible storybooks, or stories told in lesson plans, are fair renditions of the story with some useful social background, told at "an age-appropriate level." Since I am convinced that "unless you become as a little child . . . " is true, there is no such thing as an age-appropriate retelling of Bible stories. Too often the stories are watered down and moralized and, therefore, are gravely distorted with much of the real spiritual depth washed out. Remember that this method emphasizes the importance of being true to the text.

Part of the distortion might arise from curricula editors and writers who may not have grasped the implications of a particular scripture themselves. Another type of distortion arises from a lack of respect for the ability of children to understand deep spiritual realities, even if at a subliminal level they may not be able to verbalize formally. Nevertheless to "make it comprehensible for the little ones" means imposing the writer's or leader's interpretation or what he or she wants the children to get from the story, rather than letting the scripture and the questions it raises stand on their own and allowing the children to "live into the questions," as suggested in chapter 2. I cannot recommend too strongly that you simply use the Bible. Both you and the children will learn more together.

Sometimes the leaflets can be used for the amplification of the text, and occasionally for application. The pictures can be cut out to illustrate the children's own stories or for scrolls or murals or to make puppets or whatever.

But if the lesson plans are verbal/left-brained material (see chapter 1) and the whole orientation is "read the story in the Bible storybook and fill in the blanks in the leaflets," it is better for the children to make airplanes out of them. In my opinion, more children have been turned off by this kind of church school material and are no longer in the church than by almost anything else.

If you are dissatisfied with your present curriculum and prefer to adapt it rather than search for a new one, begin by following a simple lesson plan:

1. Gather with music and prayer.
2. Read the Bible lesson from the Bible.
3. Live into it by acting it out or miming it.
4. Amplify the text.
5. Express understandings and applications through arts and crafts, drama, movement, and music.
6. Close with simple worship, expressing thanks for what you have done through an offering and prayers and song.

If you happen to be primarily a left-brained thinking type, a Type-Two person according to McCarthy's delineation, find someone who is good at crafts, movement, and/or drama to help you out. That could be a teenager or an older person who needs to be released into ministry. If you spend some time each week with your helper working out your class lesson plan, going over the scripture and deciding how to do the amplification and application, both of you will learn more and will feel more relaxed with the children. A sense of community will begin to develop, and everyone will have a better time.

Don't forget the music. It is one of the most affective ways to enhance spiritual development, to "get the gospel in your gut," and to amplify a text. You will be amazed at how many people there are in churches who play musical instruments. Once I went to a small rural church to do some evaluation and leader training with its staff of four. One person played the flute and one the trombone in the local band; one was a trained outdoor education leader and one a gourmet cook, and they thought they didn't have any resources! Even if you can play a kazoo, it's a help!

If there is no one who can play an instrument, many curricula have audio cassettes, which you may play on a simple tape recorder or a boom-box. If you want special music, record it live. Simply ask the organist, or someone who plays the piano or organ or electronic keyboard with verve—and don't forget the teenagers in the rock band!—to play it, or have the choir sing it. If you have a junior choir, all the better. If not, get a group of kids together and record their singing. Younger children especially prefer those tapes. Then use the tape as the children gather and as background music while they do a craft as well as a sing-along when you need that. Once I used a tape of "For Unto Us a Child Is Born" from Handel's

Messiah during Advent with a group of children aged six through nine, even though that music is not considered age-appropriate for children that young. Nevertheless by Christmas they could all sing much of it, and they learned the Bible verse (Isa. 9:6) in the process.

Also it is not necessary to sit down to sing—actually you sing better standing up. Nor do you need to gather around the piano—or whatever. Encourage the children and allow yourself to move to the music, to make motions to express the words, to act out the ideas expressed as you sing. That way you can involve your whole being in the process—listen to and think about the words, let your body intuitively move to the music, and express your feelings as you move and sing. Such movement enhances the amplification of the text you are studying.

Here is a particularly good place to use nontraditional, alternative music, and music from different ethnic sources. One of my favorites is the "Missa Gaia" (Earth Mass) by the Paul Winter Consort, recorded live in the Cathedral of St. John the Divine, New York, and the Grand Canyon.[1] Winter's renditions of "For the Beauty of the Earth," "Song of Praise," and "The Beatitudes" are especially good. He uses wolf and loon calls and whale songs as the basis for some of the music. Moving to this piece is always an enriching experience for many people. Such movement provides some of the best application exercises. "The more we know about education and how the brain processes information, the more we understand that movement is central to learning."[2] It is also one of the most effective methods of faith development and spiritual growth.

Following the Lectionary and/or the Church Year

If only our worship service and preaching followed the same scriptures that our children are studying in church school" (or vice versa). This is another wish often expressed. If you are using a curriculum that follows the lectionary and the pastor chooses to design worship on the lectionary, then that wish, of course, will be true. There is an international, ecumenical lectionary designed by representatives of Protestant, Eastern Orthodox, and Roman Catholic churches that many churches and some curricula follow. It consists of a Psalm, an Old Testament reading, an Epistle reading, and a Gospel lesson in a three-year cycle, by which most of the Bible is read.

In the more liturgical churches—such as Roman Catholic, Eastern Orthodox, Episcopal and Lutheran—the lectionary is always followed for worship and usually so in the curricula. The Presbyterian and Reformed Educational Ministries' *Celebrate* curriculum follows the lectionary as well.

From a practical standpoint this means that the basic subject, idea, and content will be the same at worship and in church school. Consequently, families may have had similar experiences and can talk about it afterward.

Additionally, if you or the children cannot attend some Sunday you can still worship and study together. By using the TBS method you simply read one or all of the scriptures, talk and ask questions about them, act them out, draw and/or move to music, and have some silence and prayer time together. See the section "Learning at Home," which follows, for more specific instructions.

Even if the lectionary is not used, most churches follow the church year in their worship, beginning with Advent—the four Sundays before Christmas, when the emphasis is on the prophecies of the coming of a special one who would redeem Israel. Christmastide and Epiphany run until Lent, the forty days—not counting Sundays—before Easter, when the stories of Jesus' birth, ministry, sufferings of the last days, crucifixion, and death are emphasized. Then Eastertide runs until Pentecost, fifty days after Easter, when the Resurrection and post-Resurrection experiences and the beginnings of the early church are read. Pentecost then runs until Advent, from June until Thanksgiving, when any one of the lessons might be emphasized. During the summer, the Gospel lessons are often from one Gospel, reading chronologically the stories of Jesus' ministry. Usually church school curricula follow the Old Testament from September to December.

A curriculum that follows a lectionary, or at least the church year, provides an opportunity for times when the church school can participate in worship in a responsible and meaningful way. It is another form of amplification as children and leaders work through the biblical texts and very specific application as they participate in the worship. Moreover it provides wonderful training in learning how to worship as well as enabling the children to see that what they are doing has relevance to the church as a whole. It's also a form of stewardship because they are contributing something worthwhile to the worship and ministry of the church.

By using the TBS method, a class of six- to eight-year-olds could prepare the Psalm as an antiphonal reading or a choral reading with motions. A special prayer of Thanksgiving or intercession could be written by a group aged five to six. Children aged nine to twelve could prepare a dramatic reading of a scripture, and/or a modern setting of the same scripture, or they could mime while someone reads it. A group aged eleven to fourteen could prepare a call to worship using one of the scriptures and write a prayer of confession. Even a whole church school or a department in a larger church could act out the Palm Sunday story, as described in chapter 4 under "Happenings." All of these would engage the leader and the children or youth in both the amplification and the application processes.

The junior choir may prepare an introit, a choral response to prayer, a brief anthem, or a benediction based on the material they are learning. Curricula often provide such materials to be used in the classroom. Just move them into the sanctuary for worship.

By following the lectionary/church year, it is more possible for you to present meaningful programs at Christmas and for Children's Day based on material they have been studying. Again see the suggestions in chapter 4 under "Worship" and "Happenings."

Learning at Home

If only there were some way to reinforce what our children learn in church school. How can we read the Bible together at home and not have it be tedious, pious, or boring? Parents who are really concerned about their children's faith development and spiritual enrichment will often voice these wishes. Actually, the ideal place to learn together is in a family situation. It can also be a way for the family to have a brief worship time together when away on vacation or when children are ill or you're snowed in.

Our eldest son, Peter, quit going to church when he was fourteen. Now, in his thirties, he sometimes reads the Bible to his daughters as a bedtime story. Several years ago he began reading the Luke stories so the girls would understand Christmas better. Our granddaughters so enjoyed this that he began reading the Gospels to them after Christmas. We have had fascinating, transforming conversations about the meaning of various Bible passages and about how to ask significant questions that will help the girls to understand them better.

With Bible study at home it is less likely that the parents will assume that they are the "teachers" and the children are the "students." The teacher must remain a student if the teacher is to learn. The typical roles must be reversed for learning at home to work effectively.

You can use the TBS methods described in chapter 2 in a very relaxed, light, playful, fun way and have a wonderful experience. Gather in a quiet place that has as few distractions as possible. Turn on your answering machine, or take the phone off the hook if you cannot ignore it. If it is a beautiful day, go outside and gather under a tree.

If your church follows the lectionary, all the better. If not, use some of the materials your children have brought home from church school. Going through them again will help you to know what perceptions they are getting from church school. Doing a text again in a different setting will bring new illuminations and understandings. It will also reveal what the children are learning, or not learning, in church school. Or use the Gospel lesson from worship the previous Sunday and see what new thing you can learn from it through your children.

When following the lectionary, you can use part of the Psalm as a call to worship. Read the Gospel lesson as the text to study together. Then go back, and as you read each verse wonder together

What is going on here?
Why are the people doing that? Saying that?
How do you suppose so-and-so felt?
How would you have felt if you had been each of the people in the story?

Having amplified the text this way, everyone can then act out the scene. Talk about how each one felt doing his or her part. By this time some basic understandings will have emerged around the text. Think together how that might relate to each person's life.

For the application each family member could either draw a picture about how the scripture relates to her or his life or draw himself or herself into the story or think up a modern-day setting and act it out as a family. End with sharing and singing and a prayer.

One of of the most vivid and favorite church school memories of our second son, Stephen, is that of being at family camp when he was eight. For Sunday worship we acted out the Zacchaeus story (Luke 19:1-10). He was Zacchaeus and climbed a tree.

Taking time for a TBS encounter with the scripture and for deep sharing, if it can be done honestly, openly, and in a caring, learning-together mode, can deepen relationships within a family enormously. Through the power of the Holy Spirit moving among us, we all indeed become "as little children."

The One-room Schoolhouse

If only we had more room. This is another wonderful wish. But some churches are severely limited in their space, even sometimes having only a sanctuary.

In a small rural church, the two classes of twelve-to-fourteen-year-olds were taught in the sanctuary. Willis taught the boys, and I taught the girls. My voice carries, and in my excitement about the lesson it can be heard all over the lot. After a while Willis came to me and said, "Pat, the boys are listening to you rather than to me. Why don't we try teaching together?" That was a delightful solution to a bad situation—boys and girls shouldn't be separated.

"Isn't there some other place we could use?" It turned out that there was a room over the narthex that was used for storage, and we got permission to use it. He and the boys (yes, the girls should have been asked to help too!) cleaned out the room, and we all made it our own place. It also turned out to be one of the favorite meeting rooms in the church. Are you absolutely sure there is no other space?

If you have a church school of less than twenty, it is probably better for you to teach everyone together than to divide them into age groups. When you divide up that small a group, each age grouping is so tiny that you can end up with a leader, a helper, and only one child—or none on some Sundays. If people really object to this, then divide it more or less depending on how your groups shape up, by ages three to five, six to fourteen, and fourteen to eighteen. At least you lessen the pain in many small churches that have one room in which to meet, where voices compete and groups compete for the best space and someone is usually unhappy.

In order to teach diverse ages in one group, you need a leader who is good at leading Bible study, preferably according to the TBS mode, and in organizing the whole lesson plan. Then you need helpers of various ages with a variety of skills—arts and crafts, drama, movement, music. Don't forget the teenagers and the older people. Some curricula have outlines for "broadly graded classes," which provide lesson plans on how to do this kind of teaching.

If you do not have that resource, try following the basic lesson plan above. Set up the room with several tables around the edge and a circle of chairs in the middle. Place the craft materials on one table; reference books on another; Bibles, Bible storybooks, and leaflets on another; and pictures on the wall or taped to the backs of chairs *at the children's eye level.* As the children arrive have music playing and encourage them to look around the room and make some observations about what they will be doing that day. Engage them in welcoming conversation. Give those who read fairly well cards with background questions to look up in the reference books or curriculum materials. Ask one of the children, especially an older one who doesn't read well or has some learning or functional disability or is an "outsider," to run the tape recorder or to help you with some specific task.

At the appointed time, gather together for a song you may be learning. Start on time, even if only a few people are there. If you wait, the class will start later and later each week. Then remind them to get a Bible if they didn't bring theirs and gather in the circle of chairs. Begin with some sharing and a gathering prayer.

Do the Bible study together. Begin by reading the Scripture as a drama or as a dialogue or antiphonally or all together. Go through the TBS-type questions you prepared, calling on the "researchers" for pertinent information at the appropriate time. Let someone who is good at arts and crafts provide the amplification activities. Push for depth of understanding with more questions.

For application activities you can take ideas from the lesson plan and/or the leaflets and perhaps use them if they are appropriate. Or divide the group up into interest groups:

- *The arts and crafts group* could provide the backdrops, costumes, props for the drama, make a diorama, a mural, a puppet show of the story.[3] Use the Bible storybooks and leaflet pictures and materials here.

- *The drama group* could present a modern-day version of the story or act it out with costumes, or record a "you-are-there" documentary on videotape.

- *The movement group* could do an interpretation of the scripture or of the hymn, or provide an abstract modern interpretation of the Bible story. Don't forget to find out who in your church takes dancing lessons.

- *The music group* could write another verse to the hymn you are learning or prepare motions to it or learn to play it on their kazoos, rhythm instruments, or other instruments.

Sometimes it is appropriate to divide the group by age to process what they have done and to share at specific age levels. All Bible study must end up being relevant to where each person is or it is simply an interesting intellectual exercise that goes in one ear and out the other.

Divide a group of twenty or so children and youth roughly by preschool and non-readers (ages three to six), and readers (ages six/seven to ten; ten to fourteen; fourteen to eighteen). If there are no older youth (fifteen and above) divide the group into ages three to six, six/seven to nine, ten to twelve, and thirteen to fifteen. Try to be flexible, depending on the children. Sometimes there will be a situation where there are five or more children in one age level. Put them all together and divide the rest up around them. For this you will need some helpers to work with each age group, which should be one helper for every four to five children or youth. Ask people to share, demonstrate, and talk about what they have done if they are coming from interest groups. Other stimulating questions could be

How did you feel when you were doing/making this?
How did you see yourself in the Bible story? In the activity you did?
Did a situation like this ever happen to you? What did you do then?

How would you feel if you were in ——'s place?

Is there any place in your life now that is similar to what you did?

Finally, gather everyone together in the circle for a closing. This kind of teaching particularly lends itself to doing ongoing projects that give continuity and can end up with a whole church school "happening" (see chap. 4), which might be presented at worship or to parents at the end of a unit. It works particularly well if the curriculum follows the church year or is lectionary based.

The Little Box Classroom

If only we had more space! We all feel so boxed in. Many larger churches with older Christian education buildings have small classrooms for each class. A growing city church I consulted with had a separate education building with a fairly large room that would conveniently hold fifty people and little cubical classrooms around it. Each classroom had a table or two in the middle. Class sizes ranged from eight to twelve children. The noise bounced off the walls, as did some nine-year-old boys. After visiting four classes in less than an hour, I had an enormous headache.

One suggestion for dealing with the sound problem is to put cork board on the walls, on which various pictures and displays can be hung. Sound absorbing tiles on the ceiling could also help, as would insulation around the pipes.

But at least you can make the setting more tolerable by pushing the tables against the wall and laying out reference books, Bibles, leaflets, and craft materials in an interesting fashion. Then put the chairs in a circle—more or less—depending on the shape of the room. Hang on the walls pictures, dioramas, scrolls, murals, and especially felt or burlap banners or whatever the children or youth make. This provides continuity and also helps to deaden the sound.

Ask the children or youth what they think could be done with the room. They probably will come up with ideas no adult ever thought of.

Encourage the children and youth to look around as they arrive, especially if they have just come from worship. In such a situation their tendency is to plunk themselves resignedly into chairs and lean on the table in a bored manner, unless the room is inviting.

Just because the space is small, don't let it limit what you do. Make arrangements to use a bigger room or some other space for your acting-out the scripture or for movement or singing. Remember also that, weather permitting, you could go outdoors. Open the window if weather permits. If it's stuffy in the room, crack the window a little even if there's a blizzard outside.

Do everything possible to give your space an open feeling by the way you set it up, the pictures you put on the wall (large landscapes or outer space, for instance), and the open way in which you teach the class. Not everyone has to do the same thing at the same time, even in limited space. Research, arts and crafts, and small study groups can be held in different parts of the room at the same time. Small children even enjoy sitting under the table. It may mean rearranging furniture from time to time, but that in itself can be a release of energy. Let there be movement in the room and in the process of the lesson. Any of this beats sitting around a table where TBS will not happen.

Just because your classroom is boxed, you don't have to be. Let your creative energy loose. Be a child and see the situation from that perspective. Don't let "being realistic" be a cop-out for doing nothing.

Youth Work

If only we had some way to do Bible study with our youth so that they don't get bored and turned off! This plea is often heard from parents and Christian education committees. Yet, if there ever was a group that could use the TBS method and come up with unusual and often incredible insights into Scripture, it is young people. The problem is their resistance. Often their experience in church school has been so tedious and boring that they will feel they have "graduated" from that when they were confirmed and/or stopped going to Sunday school.

Yet, the closeness and sense of community that can develop within a class or within a youth group, the trust and sharing that has already taken place, can make such a group an ideal place to do TBS. However, the person leading with this method needs to have that relationship with the youth as well.

Years ago my task was to lead a fall retreat for a youth group of kids aged fifteen to eighteen. A few of the kids knew me, but not all, and the leaders were new. The purpose of the retreat was to build community. In response to my list of suggested topics for the retreat, the leaders selected "prayer." Communion with God, however was not what the kids had in mind. They saw the retreat as a chance to get away for a weekend and have some fun together, and they were definitely not interested in that heavy an input. It turned out to be something this side of a disaster. The basic problem was the lack of communication between leaders and youth about purpose and expectations. Also, the youth should have had some input into the subject of the retreat.

Another problem in using TBS with youth is that with TBS it is necessary to express and share feelings and insights, which the youth may resist. In some circumstances peer pressure and the fear of looking like a "nerd" (or whatever the current antisocial word is) will make that almost impossible. That was an added problem in the situation above.

TBS works best if the subject is something particular that is causing them to struggle. The Gospel narratives of Jesus' encounters with people are the most affective because they are short, contain a lot of action or interaction, and can be acted out and lived into more readily. Additionally they tend to deal with the issues youth face: sexuality, divorce, money, hate, love, and meaning in life. Long, convoluted theological, and often moralistic, dissertations on the Epistles are more difficult to deal with in this age group.

But given a relationship and the proper context TBS can be a wonderful experience with youth (see the experience in a church school class with Cain and Abel, p. 63).

Following is a representation of how this same group worked on the story of the of the woman at Simon the Pharisee's house (Luke 7:36-50).

L: Let's read this dramatically. Who will be the narrator? Jesus? Simon? (*A student read the passage.*) Okay. Let's take it from the top. Who, or what, was a Pharisee?

S: The religious leaders.

S: The ones who knew and interpreted the law.

S: The moral people who kept the law.

L: In our terms.

S: Members of the church board.

S: The pastor.

S: The Sunday school superintendent.

S: You! (*There was laughter at this. I nodded and laughed, too.*)

L: Why might Simon have asked Jesus to dinner?

S: To show him off to his friends.

S: To get to know him better.

S: To find out what he had to say.

L: Look at verses 37-38. What happened?

S: (*Described the woman's actions.*) How come she got in?

L: That's a good question. What was the social situation that made that possible? (*I explained that large gatherings at homes of wealthy persons were presumably open to the poor so that they could come in and pick up whatever food was thrown away.*) How were they sitting? Was she crawling around under the tables? (*laughter, comments*) Who has seen movies of Roman times? How did people sit at such parties? (*People reclined on couches.*) Why had she come? (*No response. I shifted gears.*) What kind of a woman was she?

S: A sinner. (*Several said that.*)

L: More specifically, what kind of a sinner? (*I explained that she was most probably a prostitute, largely because of the alabaster flask of ointment and her hair being down.*) What was Simon's reaction?

S1: He was upset.

S2: He thought Jesus should not have allowed her to touch him.

L: What did touching him do? (*No response. I explained that it made Jesus unclean, the food he touched unclean, and probably therefore everyone at the party unclean unless they didn't eat anything. The students thought that was pretty outrageous.*) What was another of Simon's reactions? Look at the "if" statement.

S: Does that mean he was questioning who Jesus was?

S: Was he also questioning Jesus' behavior? His awareness?

L: How did Jesus know what Simon was thinking?

S: He could probably guess what Simon's reaction would be.

L: One of the things that Jesus was always able to do, especially in his healing ministry, was to "psyche out" where people

> were coming from and what their needs and hangups were. What was Jesus' response to Simon's unspoken thought?

S: He told a story.

L: A what?

S: A parable. (*We had defined a parable before.*)

L: Will someone please retell this parable. Translate denarii into dollars. (*Someone did that.*) What is the meaning of Jesus' question at the end of the parable?

S: Boy! I'd sure love someone if he or she forgave me a debt like that!

L: But notice Simon's response—the "I suppose." What does that indicate?

S: He didn't really want to see that.

L: What contrast does Jesus make between the woman's actions in verses 44-46 and Simon's lack of social graces? Why do you suppose Simon didn't extend these courtesies to Jesus?

S: He was hedging his bets.

S: He didn't want to commit himself until he knew what kind of a person Jesus was.

L: What does Jesus mean in verse 47? Incidentally, the Greek word indicates that the words *are forgiven* should be translated "have been forgiven." That's also true for verse 48, so make the change in your Bible if you're using your own. (*I then read verse 47, properly translated.*) Which came first, the love she felt or the forgiveness?

S: The forgiveness. (*Several said that.*)

L: To whom has she expressed that love? Why? Let's go back to the earlier question of why she came in the first place.

S: She must have felt something special for Jesus.

S: Maybe she had heard him preach and knew forgiveness was possible. Maybe that's why she came.

L: Hoping for what?

S: For a new life for herself.

L: So what then is the meaning of Jesus' statement?

S: That love and forgiveness go together.

L: Why do you think Jesus makes the statement to the woman in verse 48?

S: She needed reassurance.

L: What do people hear Jesus say? What is the implication of verse 49?

S: That Jesus forgave her.

L: Did he? How does he say it? Does he say he forgives her? What specifically does he say? Forgiven by whom?

S: "Your sins are forgiven by God."

L: But the crowd hears what?

S: But he *knew* they were forgiven.

L: Right. What then does he claim?

S: To know that they were forgiven.

L: Which means he knows what?

S2: Knows that God has forgiven them.

L: And to the crowd, that's almost equally blasphemous. What then does he say to the woman?

S: "Your faith has saved you. Go in peace."

L: What does that mean? What faith?

S: Does that have anything to do with why she came in the first place? (*There was some discussion about her faith, and that Jesus could and had made a difference in her life.*)

L: What does "go in peace" mean? What was the word he would have used?

S: *Shalom.*

L: *Shalom* means what?

S: Having it all together.

L: It's very interesting that there's no conversation between Simon and the woman. Let's divide up into two groups. You guys decide what Simon would have said; the girls will decide what the woman would have said. Then we'll get together and have a conversation. (*I let them work on their own, answering questions for each group as needed. Each group chose someone to play Simon and the woman. Following is the conversation between Simon and the woman.*)

SIMON: Why did you have to come mess up my party?

WOMAN: (*offhandedly*) Sorry about that.

SIMON: Why did you have to come in like that?

WOMAN: I just had to see Jesus.

SIMON: But did you have to behave like that—weeping and (*disgustedly*) your hair down and all? What were you trying to do, embarrass me?

WOMAN: No, I told you. I just had to see Jesus.

SIMON: Look, I know I wasn't too nice the other night. My wife was away visiting her mother, and I was lonely, and—well, you know how that goes.

WOMAN: That's not the point. (*Everyone in the class assumed that Simon used the services of the woman!*)

SIMON: Well, what is the point? Why did you behave like that?

WOMAN: Because he accepted me and treated me as a human being, which is more than I can say for you the last time we were together!

L: Wow! (*Then silence.*) What then was her faith, and what is the good news she heard?

S: That Jesus accepted her as a human being.

S: He saw beyond what she was to what she might be.

S: He forgave her, and she felt like a new person.

L: What does that have to say to us about faith and the good news?

S: That God forgives us.

S: That Jesus accepts us as we are.

S: That he sees what we can become.

We ended with prayer, asking for forgiveness and giving thanks for our acceptance and for Shalom.

Unfortunately, this conversation took the whole church school hour. It would have been more affective if we had been able to paint and share that part of ourselves that needs forgiveness and transformation. That, of course, could be done in a youth group meeting or in a retreat setting where there would be more time. It could also be very affective to put on some music and let people move/dance their experience.

Incidentally, Walter Wink first did this type of Bible study with a group of bored young people in a church on the Upper West Side of Manhattan, New York City. He explains that he got tired of watching them drift off to sleep during the Sunday school lesson. So one Sunday morning in the bus on the way to the church he decided to turn the whole lesson into questions and let them figure out their own answers. The result was startling: "Over a period of two years I watched those street kids turn into rare human beings, because someone had believed they could find the truth for themselves."[4]

Chapter 4

"I Don't Do Pageants!"

Worship

Worship is the central act of the Christian church. The sabbath was originally a day of rest in remembrance that "on the seventh day God finished the work that he had done, and he rested" (Gen. 2:2). Over time it became also a day of worship. Jesus "went to the synagogue on the sabbath day, as was his custom" (Luke 4:16). After Jesus' resurrection, the disciples and others in the early church, in addition to observing the sabbath and synagogue worship, also gathered on Sunday to celebrate the resurrection and to share a common meal and communion together. As the church became less Jewish, the sabbath/synagogue observance was replaced by Sunday worship. The form of worship, or liturgy, was based on the synagogue worship, but also included readings from the letters of Paul and others; the telling of the events of Jesus' life, death, and resurrection; communion; and often a meal. When the church became legal and established in the fourth century, more formal liturgies arose, which changed with the changing times and local customs. It became institutionalized, reformed, reinstitution-alized, reformed again, bringing us to the diversity we now enjoy.

It is in this act of worship that we hear again the stories of the Hebrew Scriptures and the New Testament; sing praise to God; join in prayers of confession, thanksgiving, and intercession; participate in the sacraments of baptism and communion with our risen Lord; experience the empowering presence of the Holy Spirit; and dedicate our lives anew to love and to serve God. Remember that we call it a "service of worship."

It is important that children of all ages experience this service of worship and that they learn to participate in it rather than vegetate through it. Such participation is essential for their spiritual enrichment and faith development.

Numerous books have been written about involving children in worship.[1] Generally the emphasis is on ways to incorporate children into the worshiping community, helping them to feel at home in it.

Westerhoff emphasizes the importance of such involvement by saying: "To transmit faith to the next generation is to include them as participants in all the community's rituals."[2] An experiential emphasis will help children to become involved in worship in a meaningful way.

Transforming Bible Study is proposed as a way of reaching deeply into the experience of the listeners, so that praise and prayer are brought forth for the children to share. Naturally, the worship service is a time and place to continue with the praise and prayer that come from hearing and singing the Word.

Creating Meaningful and Inclusive Worship

Including children in worship needs to go beyond children's sermons. It involves learning the biblical language of liturgy—that is, helping them to understand the various parts of the worship service, prompting them about what will happen next and including them in what is going on. It does not mean giving them crayons or a pencil to draw on the bulletin while worship is going on. It does mean letting them find the hymns (most children can read numbers by the time they are four or even younger these days), letting the little ones stand on the pew during the singing of hymns, pointing to the words for beginning readers, inviting them to join in the prayers while avoiding the admonition to be quiet, helping them find the scripture in a Bible. In most churches children do not stay in the sanctuary for the sermon. If they do then this is the time to provide them with paper and crayons and suggest that they draw an image they may hear in the sermon or the event read in one of the scriptures or from a hymn that they sang or heard.

It is equally important that children and youth take a leadership role in worship from time to time—it is in *doing* that they learn best.

The place to begin, of course, is in the church school. Once the children have had a meaningful experience of worshiping at their level, especially if they have taken a leadership role, they can more freely participate in church worship.

In those churches where the children go to the sanctuary for the first part of the worship service, it is a good learning experience to have an occasional opening, communal worship for the whole church school. A good time to have such services is on the first

Sunday of each month, especially if that is when the church has communion. On that Sunday the children might go directly to church school and have a special worship service of their own.

It is best to begin such a practice by having this service led by someone skilled in worship. It can be a simplified version of a meaningful worship service, such as the following. By this I do not mean "opening exercises" led in by one adult in a non-participatory way with everyone sitting in rows.

The setting can be a large fellowship hall or part of a Christian education building where church school takes place. If you have a small church school that meets before or after worship and a sanctuary with choir stalls, try doing your worship there. If you hold it in a large nursery room, the little ones may crawl around on the floor or sit in people's laps. Weather permitting, try doing it outdoors, sitting on the ground.

Remember to look around for new spaces and brainstorm with leaders and youth and children for new ways to do worship. Be as creative as you can be. "We have always . . . " is usually an excuse for *not* trying something new, and "always" can sometimes turn out to be only two years.

If your church school attendance is under one hundred, arrange the room in a circle—or ellipse if the room is long and narrow. Put small chairs for small people in the first circle and build two or three circles around it. Create a worship center on the floor or a low table and reflect the theme or the season. You may, perhaps, place a candle in the center, to be lighted during each worship time to symbolize the presence of Christ, "the light of the world."

Scripture is the basis for worship and sets the theme, as does the church year, and the hymns and prayers should reflect it. The service can be a simplified version of a meaningful worship service, such as the following:

Introit and Call to Worship:
-Sung by everyone, with motions, such as "Spirit of the Living God,"[3] or

-led by a junior choir or

-led by a class or

-say part of a psalm together or

-something written and led by one class or

-something traditionally used led by a group who volunteer to do it or

-simply say, "Let us worship God."

Hymn:
-Everyone sings.

-A good time to learn a new, seasonal hymn.

-It can be led by a junior choir or

-led by a class that has been learning a particular hymn that fits the theme.

Music accompaniment could be flute, recorder, trumpet, French horn, saxophone, keyboards, guitar, or whatever—don't forget the youth in the rock band.

Bible Reading:
-Led by a leader or

-read as a drama by a class or

-acted out by a class.

Amplify and Apply:
-(This is the "sermon.") Use the TBS method of questions, conversation, acting, and/or miming with the biblical text. Where does it apply to your life today?

Offering with Music:
-Pass the baskets around the circle(s).

-Everyone sings something together or

-the junior choir sings a special song or

-a class may sing a song they have written.

-A good time to use songs suggested in the curricula.

Doxology and Prayer of Dedication:
-Whoever is leading can do a prayer or

-prayer could be led by a class.

Prayers of Intercession and Thanksgiving:
-Open to everyone. Ask "Whom or what you need to pray for today?" Celebrate birthdays, letting those who have a birthday that month stand, say their names and ages, and say "Thank you, God, for ———."

Benediction:
-Sing something together.

-Pass the peace as everyone says, "Go in peace."

After a form is established and the children become accustomed to worship, different classes may then volunteer to lead the service. This can vary from a simple "do" of the service to a drama one class may want to present based on what they have discovered from using the TBS method in their class. Allow the children to create the drama so that it is not imposed on them by a leader.

Even in small churches, or perhaps more appropriately, especially in small churches, there are opportunities for children to lead church worship. Young children can be trained to greet people as they arrive at worship, or they may usher, light candles, and receive the offering. Many of the activities they participate in during the amplification and application of the biblical text using the TBS method can be refined for use in worship. For example:

1. Lead a psalm they may have studied or learned or adapted or created motions to express their understanding.
2. Have the junior choir or a nursery or other class or the whole church school membership sing a special seasonal song they have learned or have written new words to as part of their application exercise.
3. Share prayers they have written or poems they have created, possibly with motions, to express their response to a text.
4. Act out Bible stories they have studied for the scripture reading.

In one church, each church school class attended communion at least once a year. The congregation stood in the chancel and in a large space around the communion table, and the children participated by collecting the communion cups in baskets.

It does not take much training to do any of these acts of worship. It does take commitment to helping children and youth express their understanding of the faith in a way that is meaningful to them. Such application of the scriptures, which they are encountering through TBS in church school, makes the experience relevant and significant, so that they are a vital part of the church. If this does not happen, you can count on their leaving when they are older.

Worship Is Not a Performance

Most Christmas pageants and Children's Day services do not elicit the worship of God. Stories abound of little kids and big kids and middle-sized kids forgetting memorized lines, tripping over one another to get to the chancel, dropping their props, wetting their pants, throwing up, and so on.

As the newly-hired Christian education director of a church, I was asked, "What about the Christmas pageant?" "What Christmas Pageant?" was my response. There was the usual tale of woe of lead actors who got sick, dropped props, forgotten lines, and so on. My hasty response was "I don't do pageants!" This was met by horrified silence. Then we went on to work it out.

There is a way to get around all that. Forget the memorized lines written by someone else. Forget the parades of little ones across the stage holding whatever. Forget the dropped or tripped-over props. Forget the chaos of the leads getting sick at the last minute. Forget the bathrobe parades at Christmas. Forget the advice that "when you walk down the aisle, remember to look like you're riding on a camel."

How do you get around this problem? Don't do pageants. Have a Happening.

Having Happenings

Happenings are what take place when you create a celebration through a biblical story. We celebrate an event in the life of the church or church school or a special season of the church year without making a huge production out of it. This event is similar to doing a TBS class in public. Happenings are based on the assumption that children can express in meaningful ways what the scripture says. But that depends on the manner in which the Bible is approached. Again, if we assume that children can do exegesis as described in the process of doing TBS, then that understanding can be expressed through the children's creation of Happenings.

Happenings can be done with a small class of five children or a whole church school of fifteen or fifty or one hundred fifty or five hundred or more. They can be done with little rehearsal. All they need is a good idea, using the TBS method to get at the meaning of the scripture being presented and the coordination and cooperation of a few people willing to risk.

The possibility of doing a Happening, especially if it will be done as part of worship, needs to be discussed with the pastor, the worship committee, the Christian education or church school committee, and the church school teachers, preferably several months before it is to happen. An outline with specific explanations of what will take place when and where and some basic instructions needs to be given to the leaders in advance.

The leaders may also need some help with the TBS method so that they may be enabled to elicit from the children their understanding and their expression of the scripture. The examples that follow may be of some help.

Christmas Happenings

It is possible to "grow" Christmas Happenings over the years, though they start out very simply. When people get the feel of it, the Happening can be expanded into a very meaningful presentation. Start by putting together a simple telling of the Christmas story.

Early in the fall, gather together whatever is the appropriate church school committee, the church school staff, and creative people who might help out with music, costumes, scenery, and sound. Explain to them what you want to do.

Divide the church school into age groups more or less as follows and assign parts of the story to each one:

- Ages three through five/six: Animals, birds for manger scene (Luke 2:7, 15-16).
- Ages six through eight: Shepherds (Luke 2:8-20).
- Ages nine through eleven: Wise Men, Herod, Jewish elders (Matt. 2:1-12).
- Ages twelve through fourteen: Gabriel, Mary, Joseph, donkey, Innkeeper (Luke 1:26-31, 38; 2:1-20).
- Ages fifteen through eighteen: Scripture Narrators/Readers. Some of this group might also want to use a prophecy from lectionary.

Beginning on the first Sunday in Advent, or earlier if you are going to present it as part of church worship in Advent, find out how much each class knows about the Christmas story. In preparation, each leader will need to read all of the above scriptures. Simply let each class tell the story, guiding them with question like "What happened next?" and "What about?" With younger children it is sometimes useful to "build" the story using a flannelgraph.[4]

Explain how the Happening will be put together. Each class will then read its particular story segment and will have to know its story in depth. To prepare for that ask all the questions you can think of about your class' part of the story. (For help with what kinds of questions to ask, see chap. 2, pp. 54-56, and the examples at the end of this chap.) It may also be possible to adapt your curriculum to create the Happening.

Set up a table with Bible dictionaries, atlases, concordances, and blank index cards for the students who can read to do research on specifics that may not be clear—such as who the shepherds were; why they were out on the hillside at night; what the weather may have been like; what an angel is; how far it is to Bethlehem; who Herod was; who the elders were; where wise men came from; how long it took for them to get to where Jesus was; where Nazareth and Bethlehem are; why Bethlehem was crowded; and who Gabriel, Mary, Joseph, and the innkeeper were.

In order to get into the amplification of the text, ask many *feeling* questions about the various characters: How did the shepherds feel sitting on the hillside? When they saw the angel? When they heard the multitude of the heavenly host? How would you have felt? How did Mary feel when she had to tell Joseph she was going to have a baby? How did Joseph feel? How did the wise men feel when they finally saw the star? When they arrived at the house? How did each of the people feel at the manger? How would you have felt in each instance?

With a tape recorder running have the class brainstorm the various conversations the characters might have had. Help the class to decide how each part will be acted out. You may want to go to the space to be used to find out how much room you will be able to use. Ask the class to decide what kinds of costumes to wear, and ask for outside help if necessary. They may also suggest a hymn to start or end their segment.

When each class has its segment ready, someone needs to put it all together to make sure it fits well. End each segment with an appropriate hymn for the congregation or a junior choir to sing.

The manger scene needs to be set up on a "stage." The various groups can mime the actions as the story is read, or they may act out their piece with simple dialogue they have created. Everyone needs to gather at the manger. The children who are playing animals might sing "Away in a Manger." End with everyone singing "Joy to the World."

The Happening can be done close to Christmas as a church school service, as a part of church worship, after worship in the fellowship hall, or as part of a live enactment in and through your village, town, or neighborhood on Christmas Eve. Can you come up with other possibilities that fit your special situation?

Over several years this basic plan can be expanded. Instead of using narrators and simple walk-throughs each class can create more complicated scripts. As they get more familiar with using TBS as a way of studying the scripture, the children will be able to feel into their parts of the story until they really know it.

One way to present the Christmas story is to create a puppet show. Divide each class or the group as a whole into small groups according to interest. One group of children can work on getting whatever background is needed. Others can make paper-bag puppets (small white bags donated by a friendly local bakery, or paper lunch bags, or recycled bags) for each character. These may be very simple or more fully decorated. Instead of bags, you may paste onto craft sticks pictures cut out of the curriculum materials and magazines.

Another group will write the dialogue for each segment. A group of older children can develop the narration that holds it all together. Another group can record the narration and dialogue on tape. Others can paint their parts of the "screen"—a series of white sheets or a large roll of butcher paper to hang across the front of the "stage" to hide the children and to provide a place setting for each scene. A backdrop might be painted by a mixed-age group of children, supervised by someone skilled in arts and crafts. The junior choir or any group of children may sing appropriate Christmas carols.

Someone needs to create the master script from what the children have done in class. This script will then be coordinated with the music. An older student or an adult can act as audio engineer to record on one tape all the tapes the individual groups have made, and then follow the master script to run the tape at appropriate times during the actual presentation.

This type of presentation is all prepared in advance. If someone is absent from a performance, another person will be able to substitute and work the puppet. There are no lines to be forgotten or cues to miss, as there are always coordinators (church school class leaders usually) behind the scenes to help out. Everyone is involved in some way. My experience has been that congregations are very responsive to this type of presentation.

Palm Sunday Happenings

The Palm Sunday story particularly lends itself to a whole church school Happening. If church school is held before worship the Happening can be put together that morning and then presented as the Scripture at worship. Or if the worship service and church school are held at the same time, the Happening may take place in whatever space you have for church school. If you work on the Palm Sunday Scripture the week before Palm Sunday it puts it out of sync, but presenting it the following week at worship makes it more of a performance.

When the children arrive in their classes on Palm Sunday the leader needs to explain what is going to happen. The Scripture is read and processed using the TBS mode, especially the amplification piece, so that the children understand the story. Each class is given something to shout, depending on their ages—perhaps, "Hooray for Jesus" for the youngest children to "Blessed is the kingdom of our father David that is coming" for the oldest group (see Matt. 21:9 and parallels). The children need also to understand the implication of what they are saying, which would be part of the amplification process.

Ask for volunteers from the ten to fourteen age group to be the two disciples, the person who owns the colt, and Jesus—these volunteers should not all be boys. These students will work through the scripture and create a dialogue among themselves. Then they decide where in the sanctuary or in the fellowship hall these scenes will take place.

The donkey may be acted out by (preferably, but not necessarily) a tall girl or woman with long brown hair pulled through a paper-bag donkey head, and wearing a tan sweater, slacks, and boots. Also an "elder" from the congregation can be invited to be the Pharisee who confronts Jesus. This whole process of preparation usually takes about twenty minutes.

The coordinator then gathers everyone together. If the Happening is going to be done as scripture during the worship service, it is now run through, in the sanctuary if possible, to make sure that all the children are aware of what they are doing, to iron out glitches, and to make sure that the children feel comfortable with the idea that they are doing the scripture for worship. Or it simply "happens" as part of the church school session.

At the appropriate time palms are handed out to everyone. The pastor, reader, or coordinator begins reading or telling the Palm Sunday story. The story then unfolds or happens with everyone involved as the scripture describes it. As "Jesus" passes along among the waving branches the children *shout* their lines. If the Happening is done as a worship service, you may end by having the choir or congregation sing Faure's "The Palms" or some other appropriate and familiar anthem or hymn.

If your Happening is done as part of the church school session or if you return to church school after the Happening, you need to process what happened. Ask the children such questions as: How did you feel? Were you surprised at what happened? What happened next?"If there is time each class might discuss what happened following Palm Sunday during Holy Week.

A month or so after doing such a Happening during church school at a suburban church, one of the leaders came to see me and brought her five-year-old son with her. I asked the little boy to excuse us while we talked and gave him some books to look at and a puzzle to do. After about ten minutes he said, "Oh, wow!" I asked him what he had seen. He excitedly brought the book to me, showed me a picture, and proudly stated, "That's Palm Sunday!"

Church School/Children's Day Happenings

Happenings work particularly well for end of church school celebrations or for Children's Day programs. The curriculum at this time of year is often based on the book of Acts. Instead of having each class do the lesson/scriptures assigned for each week, divide the various stories among the classes according to what interests each leader or what seems appropriate for each class. Then each class works on its story in depth, using the TBS process. Most of the stories in Acts are not well known and are often long and involved. It is better to do one thoroughly than to half understand a series of stories.

Several of the stories about Saul/Paul can be done under the title "Following in the Footsteps of Paul." Some of the scripture segments that you may choose to use as scenes in the story are Stephen and Saul (Acts 6:8–8:3), Saul's Damascus Road experience (Acts 9:1-9), Paul and Ananias (Acts 9:10-19), Paul and the disciples (Acts 9:20-31), and Paul and Silas in prison (Acts 16:6-12, 16-34 see the accessing questions below.)

To join the segments together, use hymns or various verses of one hymn, such as "Faith of Our Fathers," with verses the children have written to tell their story. These can be sung by the classes to end or to introduce their stories, by all the children, by a children's choir, by the combined junior and adult choirs, or by the whole congregation.

Another possibility is to use Avery and Marsh's "The Great Parade" with stories about Philip and the eunuch (Acts 8:4-9, 26-40), Barnabas (Acts 4:27-32; 9:26-27; 15:22-37), the church at

Antioch (Acts 11:19-30) and Lydia (Acts 16:11-15, 40), and Paul and Silas in prison (Acts 16:6-12, 16-34).[5]

The following is an example of how you develop a Happening segment from Acts 16:16-34 to tell the story of Paul and Silas in prison.

Verse 16. Who is "we"? (See vv. 1 and 14. Perhaps it is Luke, the author? Since this is probably a conflation of several incidents it is sometimes hard to tell who is being talked about.) Where are they? (See v. 12. Do map research.) Where was the place of prayer? (See v. 13.) Did they seem to know where they were going? What to expect? What kind of a situation did that set up? Who were they met by? What did she do? What is a soothsayer? (Do research in Bible dictionary.)

Verse 17. What did she do? What is she saying? How do you suppose Paul and the others felt? How would you have felt? What would you have done?

Verse 18. What happens? Why do you suppose Paul was annoyed? Would you have been? What does he do? What would you have done? Why? What was the understanding about spirits? (The understanding at the time was that anyone who had extraordinary gifts had them through some spirit, just as we understand that people have unusual mystical awareness through the power of the Holy Spirit. It is also similar to our understanding of intuitional and other extrasensory abilities, such as ESP, which we now know can be either inhibited or trained.) What happens to the spirit?

Verse 19. What was her owners' reaction? What did they do? Where did they take Paul and Silas? Why? What's the set-up here?

Verses 20-21. What accusation did her owners make? What are the social implications? Had Paul and Silas actually broken a law? What had they done? Look again at verses 18 and 19.

Verse 22. What is going on here? Then what happens? What do the magistrates do?

Verse 23. What happens? Notice what the magistrates command the jailer to do. Why?

Verse 24. What was the jailer's response to this command? Does that really seem necessary? Why did he do that?

Verse 25. What was Paul and Silas's response to being in prison? Is that surprising? Would you have done that? What would you have done? (Push a little for them to answer honestly.)

Verse 26. Then what happens? Do you think God caused the earthquake, or that it was synchronistic, or that Paul and Silas were just lucky?

Verse 27. What was the jailer's response? Why did he do that?

Verse 28. What was Paul's response? Is that surprising? Why didn't he and Silas just take off?

Verses 29-30. What was the jailer's response? Why? What had happened to him? (Talk about this a bit.)

Verse 31. What does this mean? How do you suppose the jailer heard and understood it? Do you?

Verse 32. Where had they gone? What do you suppose Paul and Silas said?

Verses 33-34. What was the jailer's response? How was he feeling? His family? Paul and Silas?

Once the story is clear to the children, have them act it out. It's really not as long or complicated as it seems. It will help everyone to feel into the situation better and thereby amplify the text.

For application go back to verses 25 and 30-32.

Verse 25. Have you ever felt as if you were in prison? What were the circumstances? How did you feel? What did you do? How did you respond? Would you have prayed? Sung? Why or why not? Could that have helped? Can you think of a situation where it might?

Verse 30. Since you are baptized Christians (I'm assuming infant baptism here), you are already part of the household of God. (If your church practices believer's baptism or you were never baptized simply ask the following question.) What does "believing in the Lord Jesus" mean for you, especially in the light of verse 25?

Verse 31. What would you have said?

Have each class or a special group or the junior choir, *not a leader or other adult,* write a verse to describe each event, which is then sung to introduce each segment in the presentation. The congregation or the whole church school sings the refrain "Come Join the Great Parade," from "The Great Parade," as a bridge to the next scene.

Then come up with some way to present the Happening—live, puppets, slides, videotape. The presentation can be shared as the scripture and sermon in a worship service. Those not participating in the actual presentation can be called on to assist with other parts of the service, which of course will be designed around the Happening.

A Happening sure beats the usual "show-and-tell" performances that have sometimes traditionally taken place on Church School Day. Some people may find such a performance cute and sweet, but it is hardly worship. The biggest problem in creating a Happening is dealing with the parents who, for sentimental and emotional reasons, want to replicate their experiences on Church School Day. However, their particular experiences are usually not good worship, and if you really listen to their tales of what they did as children, you will find that their experiences are often not very positive to say the least. Some adults may have learned to laugh at themselves for the silly things they recited and the goofs they made, but is that what they want to subject their children to? If you can say that you want the Children's Day service not to be a "show-and-tell" or a performance, but real worship, you may get away with a Happening. And once you've done it, you'll never go back!

Pentecost Happenings

Pentecost, which is often a day of celebration, offers an appropriate opportunity to create a worship service for the end of the church school or Children's Day. Such services often coincide with Pentecost in the church calendar and common lectionary. Church school curricula that follow the lectionary or are based on the church year will often have suggestions for Pentecost celebrations.

The scripture to use for Pentecost is Acts 2:1-15. For class use, unless you have teenagers and lots of time, read verses 1-8*a* and 11*b*-15.

> *Verse 1.* What was Pentecost? (Have someone look it up in a Bible dictionary. See also Lev. 23:15-21.) Who are "they"? (See 1:13*b*-15.) Where were they? (See 1:12-13*a*.) Why? (See 1:4-5.) How might they have been feeling?
>
> *Verse 2.* What happened? How do you suppose they felt about that? Remember that the words *wind, breath,* and *Spirit* are derived from the same word (*ruach* and *pneuma*) in Hebrew and in Greek.

Verse 3. Then what happens? What feelings might people have had? What would you have felt?

Verse 4. What do you suppose it means to be "filled with the Holy Spirit?" What feelings might people have had? What happens?

Verse 5. Why were the Jews in Jerusalem? Where had they come from? (See verses 8*b*-11*a*; have some students do map research for this answer.) Why had they come so far? (Use information gathered.)

Verse 6. Why did they all come together? Why were they bewildered? What other words might you use to describe their feelings? (Slang is helpful here.)

Verse 7. How did they know they were Galileans? (More map research. Remember it's the area Jesus and the disciples came from.)

Verses 8a and 11b. Here I usually tell the story of going to an installation service many years ago for a young Italian-speaking pastor in a Italian-speaking church. The installing pastor was very pompous and preached a very boring sermon—and that's all I remember about it. But the old retiring Italian-speaking pastor preached a very moving sermon in Italian, which I don't speak, but could follow from my knowledge of Latin, French, and Spanish. I understood him to say that just having a young, new pastor would not bring that church alive again. What was needed was for everyone to be aware of the power of the Holy Spirit in his or her life. It was one of the most moving sermons I have ever heard. Have you ever heard something beautiful and meaningful even if you didn't understand the words? What about great choral music? What are other possibilities?

Verse 12. What does this mean?

Verse 13. Who might have said this? What did he or she mean?

Verses 14-15. Why Peter? What time was it? (About 9:00 A.M. Do research here; the day started at sunrise, about 6:00 A.M.)

For amplification get into the underlying meaning and feeling and don't try to answer all the imponderable questions—live them instead by acting it out. Encourage everyone to get into the act. We cannot appreciate this passage by sitting and analyzing it.

For application brainstorm about how to symbolize what happened. What happens to a balloon when you blow it up (have some balloons around to play with). Cut out "flames" from red, yellow, and orange crepe paper, cellophane, or construction paper. Make a Pentecost tree.[6] What about wind? And your breath? Can you see them? How do you know they are there? Have you ever had a similar experience of the Holy Spirit in your life? The reason no one ever talks about such experiences is because no one ever takes the possibility seriously enough to ask the question.

From all the insights of all the classes, the leaders can put together an acting out of the Pentecost story, then build a worship service around it. For example:

Introit:
-The junior choir or the entire church school could sing "Spirit of the Living God" with motions (see note 4).

Call to Worship:
-From the balcony or the back of the church or from all over people could say, "Receive God's Spirit!" Or they may say the first "creed" of the church, "Jesus is Lord," in different languages. (Oh, yes you can!)

Opening/Processional Hymn:
-Unfortunately there are not many celebratory Pentecost hymns. Sing something rousing with a lot of alleluias in it—even an Easter hymn or "Praise the Lord, God's Glories Show." During the hymn, the children could bring in the Pentecost tree and put it in front of the pulpit or some other appropriate place.

Opening/Prayer of Confession:
-The pastor or a church school leader may lead in prayer, or this prayer may be something a class has done that came out of their study. It could include a confession of the reality that we don't usually tune in to the Holy Spirit.

Scripture:
-The Old Testament lesson could be Joel 2:28-33, which Peter quotes in Acts 2:17-21. It could be done antiphonally by a group aged eight to eighteen, who prepared it as a special activity. Acts 2 could be acted out or mimed as it is read. The younger children can distribute among the congregation the "flames" they made.

Offering:

-You may choose to distribute the flames now instead of earlier. A junior choir, a special group of children, or the whole church school could sing "We Are the Church."[7]

Hymns:

-One traditional one wouldn't hurt, such as "Breathe on Me, Breath of God" or "Spirit of Gentleness" or another from your hymnal. Or you may use a folksong or sing in a Plainsong mode "Come Holy Spirit Our Souls Inspire."

Benediction:

-Try singing one. The new Presbyterian hymnal has an arrangement of "May the Lord, Mighty Lord" sung to a Chinese folk tune.

The primary ingredient in all Happenings is simply to let the kids be themselves. It works best where classes are taught in the open TBS way, described in chapter 2.

Trust the children's ability to apprehend the importance of worship. Allow them to be responsible for important tasks and respect their ability to do so. Once the "right answer" syndrome has been removed and they are freed to be themselves and to express their wonder and amazement at the power of Scripture in their lives, many wonderful things can happen. Have Happenings!

Vacation Church School

Perhaps the most effective place to start trying some of these TBS methods is in VCS or VBS. One or two whole weeks of three-hour sharing times lend an intensity and continuity not available in church school. At one suburban church I worked with, the attendance started out at eighty and went to ninety by the end of the week—people were having so much fun they brought friends. The theme was "God's Good Creation."

Several weeks before VCS began, a day-long retreat for all the leaders was held. How to do the curriculum in a meaningful way was one of the chief concerns. My leading these leaders through an experience of TBS, using one of the scripture lessons to be used at

VCS, influenced these leaders to make the commitment to try the method with their classes.

The creative activities were devised on the basis of the curriculum and provided by two women who are terrific with crafts. Snacks were provided by parents, coordinated by one parent who particularly liked doing that.

The leaders met each morning at 8:30 for announcements, sharing of problems, and centering. Babysitting was provided for the leaders' children during this time and for their children who were under three years old for the entire week. At 9:00 A.M., singing began as people gathered, lasting until about 9:15. Then the children were divided into age groupings for Bible study, games, and crafts.

Bible study was done with everyone sitting in circles, based on the TBS method. I led the Bible study in a class of children aged eight to eleven, which had eighteen to twenty-two members. This class was used as a training session for two other leaders whose main responsibilities were to give leadership to the crafts and games, which were all related to the amplification and application of the Scripture. The games were all cooperative.[8]

Snacks (crackers and fruit juice—no sugar; the kids were hyperactive enough!) were taken to each group at appropriate times by a group of volunteers. Everyone gathered at 11:45 for closing worship in which groups who wished to do so shared something they had done.

On Friday the parents were invited to join us for a closing worship at 11:30, followed by a simple lunch, again provided by volunteers. This worship was a culmination and expression of our learning and experiences during the week.

As quiet music was played, the entire VCS gathered in the big room of the church. The call to worship each morning, "This Is the Day," was sung by everyone. The prayer of confession was written by the eight- to eleven-year-old group.[9] It was their response to the Bible study on the creation story (Gen. 1), using the TBS method they had experienced. All the leaders sang a special song. A play on the Creation was presented by the second-grade group. An adaptation of Psalm 8 was recited with motions by a small group of the eight to eleven year olds.[10] We sang "For the Beauty of the Earth," which we had learned during the week. An offering, which netted $85, was taken among the parents for the poor of the world while the children presented a symbolic craft they had made, then we sang the doxology. Prayers of thanksgiving were led by the kindergarten group, and an intercessory prayer was led by the first-grade group. The benediction was sung by everyone.

Here again meaningful worship arose from the experiences of the week. Involvement was negotiated, not assigned. The children expressed their understanding in their own words and with their arts and crafts. They were familiar with what they were doing, and the worship simply flowed. Many parents expressed amazement at the children's ability to participate so freely and enthusiastically in the worship. The entire week was a wonderful learning experience for everyone—it simply happened.

By contrast, one summer Sunday my husband was leading worship and preaching at a small rural-becoming-suburban church. A laywoman led the first part of the service, including the "children's sermon." About a half-dozen children came down front, and she asked them questions about what they had done in VCS the week before. No one said a word. So she proceeded to go through each day of the week, reminding them of what they had learned.

What a missed opportunity! If only she, or whoever had led the VCS for the church, had seen what could have happened. Those children were perfectly capable of having created that first part of the worship service themselves by expressing in their own way in a psalm, a song, and prayers that they had studied, created, and learned.

Examples

An Intergenerational Worship Service

One of the best experiences I have had in helping children to learn how to experience the Bible in worship happened many years ago in a city church in a changing community. It was decided that there needed to be two worship services, with church school in between. The church school curriculum was based on the lectionary, from which the pastor also preached.

The early service lasted only a half-hour, but it was a full, liturgical worship service. Initially it was attended mostly by young families, the young people, and the church school students and leaders. Sometimes one of the hymns was a folk hymn. The scripture was read, and the sermon was a five-minute exposition on the scripture. The offering was received by the families or youth who were serving as ushers. During the doxology our three-year-old Timothy stood on the pew, singing at the top of his lungs.

Instead of a pastoral prayer there was a prayer of intercession. The pastor asked, "Whom or what do you want to pray for?" The children and some adults would respond with "My grandmother is in the hospital"; "The astronauts"; "The family whose house burned down last night"; "I'm having my tonsils out tomorrow"; "The people who were hurt in the hurricane in"; and so on. It was always amazing to me to see how aware the children were of what was going on about them. This was followed by a prayer of thanksgiving, which was printed in the bulletin. After a month or so all the children knew the prayer by heart.

It was basically a traditional church. Surprisingly, after about three months there were more people at the early service than the late one—the early service was called "the swinging thing" and the later "the quiet box." But some people felt that two churches were being created. So it was decided that for one Sunday the church school would be held first, and then we would have one worship service and a special festal coffee hour.

The older people who usually attended the second service were amazed at how well the children participated in the worship. At the coffee hour many children were complimented on how well they behaved in church—which most of them thought was a dumb remark. Then one older man said it all, "Why, they seemed to understand what was going on better than I did." Obviously, their experience in worship made that possible.

Perhaps even more significant, at dinner that day our ten-year-old son, Peter, said, "Dad, don't ever do that again!" In response to his father's astounded "What?" and "Why?" Peter said, "Because we had church school first instead of worship, we had to spend the whole time in class reading and understanding the Bible story, and we never got to *do anything creative about it!*"

Creative Christmas Happenings

The following are two of my favorite conversations that were part of a Christmas Happening puppet show. The first is between two youth aged twelve and thirteen who recreated how Mary may have told Joseph she was going to have a baby.

Mary and Joseph

M: (*hesitantly*) Uh, Joseph. . . .
J: Yes, Mary.
M: Uh . . . I have something to tell you.
J: Yes, what?
M: Uh . . . I'm going to have a baby.
J: *You're what?*
M: (*very matter-of-factly*) I am going to have a baby.
J: That's impossible.
M: I know.
J: But . . . but. . . . Who's the father anyway? Have you been fooling around?
M: (*pleadingly*) Joseph.
J: Okay. But. . . . (*total exasperation*) I don't understand!
M: Well, an angel named Gabriel came to me. . . .
J: Aw come on, Mary.
M: No really, the angel Gabriel came to me and told me that I was going to have a baby by the power of the Holy Spirit and that we should name him Jesus.
J: That's the most ridiculous story!
M: But, Joseph, it's true!
J: I can't accept that.
M: (*The small, shy twelve-year-old girl who played* MARY *said the following with great centeredness and determination.*) That's too bad!

The other conversation was about Herod's giving directions to Bethlehem to the wise men, played by children aged ten to twelve. Herod was played by a ten-year-old student who sometimes acted up in class.

Herod to the Wise Men

WISE MEN: How do we get to Bethlehem?
HEROD: You go out the castle grounds, take a left, go through the gate, take a right and go about five miles down the road to Bethlehem. And don't forget to come back and tell me where he is!

This happening went without a hitch. Everyone was amazed at the depth of understanding of "these little children." Their teacher said, "I thought I knew the story of the wise men, but when we began really working on it, I discovered I knew hardly anything at all!"

Another and rather unusual Christmas Happening took place at a 350 member suburban church with a church school of about 85 members. The TBS method of Bible study was generally used throughout the church school. A young father who sang, played the guitar and synthesizer, wrote music, and had all sorts of audio equipment in his basement was very committed to the church and offered to begin a junior choir.

He and the fifteen choir members, aged eight to twelve, wrote a musical play titled *God Is Still Creating.* Each week at choir rehearsal they put together another segment based on what they had studied in their church school classes the Sunday before. Don wrote the music and the words to the songs based on what the kids had talked about. The dialogue was essentially written by the kids. The scenes were titled "Creation," "Flood, Flood, Flood," "Thanksgiving," "God's Mysterious Ways," "The Magnificat" (read by junior highs students and danced by a thirteen-year-old girl), "Incarnation," and "God Is Still Creating"—"creating through you, creating through me, God is still creating."

The musical was presented as the scripture and sermon on the third Sunday in Advent, with the entire church school at worship. It ended with a tableau of the manger scene. A young couple who had a one-month-old baby portrayed the Holy family. A triptych behind them in the chancel was painted by the ten- to twelve-year-old class. An eleven-year-old played the donkey, a nine-year-old the annunciation angel, and several smaller angels were played by children aged six to seven. Five five-year olds played the animals around the manger (in pajamas and Halloween costumes). A "lion" and a "lamb," also five-year-olds, sat together on the edge of the stage at the foot of the manger.

As "Mary" laid her baby in the manger, the senior choir began singing "For Unto Us a Child Is Born" from Handel's *Messiah.* The scene continued to be created. Then each child in the church school placed in front of the manger a gift for needy children in the near-by city. As the last child left the chancel, the choir ended the anthem. This was neither timed nor planned—it simply happened synchronously and serendipitously. Then there was an awesome silence. As a hymn was sung the children returned to sit with their parents.

Again the reaction was one of amazement at the depth of commitment, understanding, and reverence with which the worship was presented. My husband commented at the end of "God Is Still Creating," "That was some of the best theology I've heard in a long time."

Children's Day Worship

On Children's Sunday at a downtown church where I was the Education Consultant, we integrated all sixty children aged three and older in the church school into the regular morning worship service. One twelve-year-old young man was very artistic and designed the cover for the bulletin—several balloons with "O Happy Day!" written underneath. The church school staff and the Christian education committee liked it so much they decided to provide bright blue t-shirts with that logo and the name of the church to the church school staff and the children, who were asked to wear them over white shirts.

After the prelude the organist played some quiet "walking in" music as all the children and staff, carrying balloons, entered from the many doors into the sanctuary and gathered in the chancel. The congregation, normally rather staid, broke into spontaneous applause. As a call to worship the children and the adult choir sang "This Is the Day" antiphonally. When the children left the chancel to sit with their parents, they put their balloons on the edges of the pews down the center aisle (and one pink one on the organ in the chancel!)

Some of the older children, the youth, and the leaders participated in the service. The pastor's sermon emphasized the whole family of the church. All the children sang Avery and Marsh's "I Am the Church" with motions as the offertory anthem.

Afterward the pastor commented that the church school members had obviously been working toward this for some time, and it showed the dedication and creativity of all of us. It was followed by a wonderful ice cream social on the lawn. The comments from the entire church were very positive and again reflected their amazement at the ability of the children and youth to participate so meaningfully in adult worship.

Making such experiences possible all goes back to our understanding about children. Are we going to allow them to be participatory members of the congregation or continue to expect them silently and obediently to vegetate through worship and give "right answers" in church school? Are we going to continue to assume that they don't know anything and have to be spoonfed? Or are we going to believe, as Jesus did, that "unless you become as a little child, you shall not enter the [Realm] of God"?

If after leafing through or reading this book you feel totally intimidated and say, "I couldn't possibly do that!" know that I understand. Although I took to Transforming Bible Study like a duck to water, I have worked with enough people who feel overwhelmed to appreciate that feeling.

Or if you are already working with a method similar to this mode of learning, feel alone and strange and need affirmation and hope, know that I've been there myself and understand how you feel.

To each of you I would say:

- Trust yourself—your innate childlike wonder and excitement about new ideas and possibilities.
- Trust the children—their openness, responsiveness, and natural curiosity and creativity.
- Trust the process—TBS has been used creatively and powerfully by many people in many situations for many years.
- Trust God—for therein is the basis of your faith.
- Trust Jesus—who said, "Where two or three are gathered in my name, I am there among them" (Matt. 18:20).
- Trust the Holy Spirit—to empower you to do this work well.

Remember that the bottom line is "unless you become as a little child. . . ."

1. "Unless You Become . . . "

1. A paradigm is a pattern or form.

2. Throughout this book I use affective, rather than effective, to mean that the experience and the learning do not simply produce a decided, decisive, or desired effect and are efficient and efficacious. Rather, they affect the way we perceive, feel, and respond to the biblical passage and the learning process. They produce feelings, emotions, and desires that determine our thought and conduct. By affecting the way we perceive and feel, they change the way we behave.

3. The right hemisphere of the brain dominates the left side of the body. It is concerned with spacial relations and has a simultaneous time sense. Its thinking functions are synthetic, imaginative, holistic, acausal, and metaphorical. It expresses itself in music (untrained), drawing, depth perception, and complex visual patterns. It controls gestures and facial expressions, and recognizes faces, shapes, sizes, colors, textures, and forms. It operates during our sleep/dreaming state, meditation, and ESP. It dominates the life of the artist, the inventor, and the innovator.

The left hemisphere dominates the right side of the body. It is concerned with temporal relations and has a linear time sense. Its thinking functions are analytical, logical, abstract, sequential, and cause and effect. It expresses itself in speech, grammar, naming, math, and trained musical expressions. It dominates the life of the logician, the engineer, the critic, and the analyst.

For a description of how knowledge of the functions of the hemispheres of the brain makes an impact on our study of the Bible see Walter Wink, *Transforming Bible Study,* 2nd ed. (Nashville: Abingdon Press, 1989), pp. 22-36.

4. John Westerhoff H. III, *Will Our Children Have Faith?* (New York: Seabury Press, 1976), pp. 9-22.

5. Michael P. Grady, *Teaching and Brain Research: Guidelines for the Classroom* (New York: Longman, 1984), p. 7.

6. Ibid., p. 102.

7. Ibid., p. 103.

8. Bernice McCarthy, *The FourMat System: Teaching to Learning Styles with Right-Left Mode Techniques* (Barrington, Ill.: Excel, 1980), pp. 37-43.

9. Ibid., p. 49.

10. Rainer Maria Rilke, *Letters to a Young Poet,* trans. M. D. Herter Norton (New York: W. W. Norton, 1954), pp. 34-35.

11. See Arlene J. Ban, *Teaching and Learning with Older Elementary Children* (New York: Judson Press, 1979) and Edgar Dale, "Dale's Cone of Learning," adapted by Helen Tetley, ed. *Five Designs for Teacher/Leader Education* (Louisville: Presbyterian Publishing House, 1989).

12. Parker Palmer, *The Promise of Paradox: A Celebration of Contradictions in the Christian Life* (Notre Dame: Ave Maria Press, 1980), pp. 111-25.

13. Ibid., p. 116.

14. Ibid.

15. Ibid., p. 117.

16. See Andy LePage, *Transforming Education: The New Three R's* (Oakland, Calif.: Oakmore House Press, 1987), p. 52.

17. Ibid., p. 54; italics added.

18. A wonderful resource is Michael J. Caduto and Joseph Bruchac, *Keepers of the Earth: Native American Stories, with Environmental Activities for Children,* with a teacher's guide (Golden, Colo.: Fulcrum, 1988). Michael J. Caduto also does workshops for students and educators, in which he teaches the culture, stories, music, and dance of many Native American nations. Write to Environmental and Cultural Education, Michael Caduto, P. O. Box 1052, Norwich, VT 05055, (802) 649-1815.

19. Sue Bredecamp, ed., "Developmentally Appropriate Practice in Early Childhood: Programs Serving Children from Birth Through Age 8," *Young Children,* National Association for the Education of Young Children (1988): 64-68, 81-84.

20. Patricia H. Bern with Eve Bern, "Nurturing Success," *Pre-K Today,* Scholastic, Inc. (August/September 1988): 33-37, 54.

21. See Marjorie J. Kostelnik, Laura C. Stein, and Alice P. Whiren, "Children's Self-Esteem: The Verbal Environment," *Childhood Education,* Association for Childhood Education International (Fall 1988): 29-32.

22. See James W. Fowler, *Stages of Faith: The Psychology of Human Development and the Quest for Meaning* (San Francisco: Harper & Row, 1981) and *Becoming Adult, Becoming Christian* (San Francisco: Harper & Row, 1984).

23. See Lawrence Kohlberg, *The Philosophy of Moral Development* (San Francisco: Harper & Row, 1981).

24. See Susan Johnson, *Christian Spiritual Formation in the Church and Classroom* (Nashville: Abingdon Press, 1989), pp. 108-11.

25. Westerhoff, *Will Our Children Have Faith?* pp. 50-51.

26. Ibid., p. 85.

27. See Jack Canfield and Harold Wells, *100 Ways to Enhance Self-concept in the Classroom* (Englewood Cliffs, N.J.: Prentice-Hall, 1976); Fran Schmidt and Alice Friedman, *Creative Conflict Solving for Kids,* ages nine to fourteen (Miami: Grace Contrino Abrams Peace Education Foundation, 1986); Fran Schmidt and Alice Friedman, *Fighting Fair for Kids* (Miami: Grace Contrino Abrams Peace Education Foundation, 1986); James Muro and Don Dinkmeyer, *Counseling in the Elementary and Middle Schools: A Pragmatic Approach* (Dubuque: William C. Brown, 1987); Anderson, *Thinking, Changing, Rearranging;* See Bible-o-graph; DUSO Kits: *Developing Understanding of Self and Others,* Circle Pines, MN. American Guidance Series, 1970.

28. Madeline L'Engle, *Trailing Clouds of Glory: Spiritual Values in Children's Books* (Louisville: Westminster John Knox, 1985).

29. Charles L. Whitfield, *Healing the Child Within* (Deerfield Beach: Health Communications, Inc., 1987), pp. 8, 127.

30. See Jeremiah Abrams, ed., *Reclaiming the Inner Child* (Los Angeles: Jeremy P. Tarcher, 1990).

31. See Joan Borysenko, *Guilt Is the Teacher, Love Is the Lesson* (New York: Warner Books, 1990); *Minding the Body, Mending the Mind* (New York: Bantam Books, 1988). She also gives workshops throughout the country.

32. Peter Kline, *The Everyday Genius: Restoring Children's Joy of Learning* (Arlington: Great Ocean Publishers, 1989), cited in *Brain/Mind Bulletin,* 14, 8 (May 1989): 4.

33. Glen Bannerman, *APCE Advocate,* 14, 1 (March 1989): 1.

34. See Judy Gattis Smith, *Teaching to Wonder: Spiritual Growth Through Imagination and Movement* (Nashville: Abingdon Press, 1989); *Developing a Child's Spiritual Growth Through Sight, Sound, Taste, Touch, and Smell* (Nashville: Abingdon Press, 1983).

35. Iris V. Cully, *Education for Spiritual Growth* (San Francisco: Harper & Row, 1984), p. 157.

36. Jiyu Kennett, Roshi, *Zen Meditation* (Mt. Shasta: Shasta Abbey Press, 1980), p. 8.

37. Frances Vaughan, *The Inward Arc: Healing and Wholeness in Psychotherapy and Spirituality* (Boston: Shambala, 1986), p. 19.

38. Frances Vaughan, *Awakening Intuition* (Garden City, N.Y.: Doubleday, 1979), p. 63.

39. John H. Westerhoff III and John D. Eusden, *The Spiritual Life: Learning East and West* (New York: Harper & Row, 1982), pp. 2-3.

40. Ibid., p. 3.

41. Ibid., pp. 47-48.

42. Sue Comstock, "Nurturing the Spiritual Experience of Children," *Church Educator* (February 1985).

43. Westerhoff, *Will Our Children Have Faith?* p. 83.

44. Pat Rodegast and Judith Stanton, *Emmanuel's Book* (New York: Bantam, 1987), p. 60.

2. Getting the Gospel in Your Gut

1. Walter Wink, *Transforming Bible Study*, 2nd ed. (Nashville: Abingdon Press, 1989), p. 42.

2. Parker Palmer, *To Know As We Are Known: A Spirituality of Education* (San Francisco: Harper & Row, 1983), pp. 98-99.

3. Robert McAfee Brown, *The Bible Speaks to You* (Louisville: Westminster John Knox, 1985), p. 87.

4. Wink, *Transforming Bible Study*, p. 40.

5. Ibid.

6. Thomas Keating, *The Heart of the World* (New York: Crossroads, 1981), pp. 45-46.

7. Wink, *Transforming Bible Study*, p. 38.

8. Ibid., p. 39.

9. *Synchronistic* means happening at the same time, as in "synchronize your watches." Here it implies that at the same time a number of different people will all come up with a new way of expressing the same idea, each in a different and meaningful way.

10. *Synergistic* means the cooperative action of several people or events so that the total effect is greater than the sum of the two effects by themselves, or the whole is greater than the sum of the parts. Here it implies that people working together can produce a result far greater than the total of each of them working independently.

11. The word *hologram* is derived from the Greek words *holo*, meaning "whole" and *gram* meaning "to write." Thus the hologram is an instrument that, as it were, "writes the whole." See David Bohm, *Wholeness and the Implicate Order* (London: Routledge & Kegan Paul, 1980), p. 145. We see holograms as three-dimensional images or "pictures" on magazines, credit cards, and trinkets. When placed in a strong light they become illuminated and seem to "move" as we move them around. In amplifying the scripture we create a more whole image of the biblical passage.

12. Wink, *Transforming Bible Study*, p. 39.

13. See Patricia Griggs, *Opening the Bible with Children: Beginning Bible Skills* (Nashville: Abingdon Press, 1986); Donald Griggs, *Twenty New Ways of Teaching the Bible* (Nashville: Abingdon Press, 1979); Judy Gattis Smith, *Twenty-six Ways to Use Drama in Teaching the Bible* (Nashville: Abingdon Press, 1988); Boyd Lein, *Journey to Jerusalem* (Nashville: Abingdon Press, 1987); Dorothy Jean Furnish, *Experiencing the Bible with Children* (Nashville: Abingdon Press, 1990); Lois M. Runk, *Working with Elementary Children* (Nashville, Discipleship Resources, 1989); Roger A. Gobbel and Gertrude G. Gobbel, *The Bible: A Child's Playground* (Philadelphia: Fortress Press, 1986).

14. Wink, *Transforming Bible Study*, p. 82.

15. Ibid., p. 40.

16. Ibid., pp. 77, 78.

17. Burton H. Throckmorton, Jr., ed., *Gospel Parallels: A Synopsis of the First Three Gospels* (Nashville: Thomas Nelson, 1979).

18. For more on the gnostic gospels, see Elaine Pagels, *The Gnostic Gospels* (New York: Vintage Books, 1981), especially the Introduction.

19. Wink, *Transforming Bible Study*, p. 95.

20. Henri J. M. Nouwen, *The Wounded Healer* (Garden City, N.Y.: Doubleday, 1972), p. 41.

3. "If Only We Had . . . "

1. Paul Winter, "Missa Gaia" (Litchfield, Conn.: Living Music Records, Inc., 1982).

2. Teresa Benzwie, *A Moving Experience: Dance for Lovers of Children and the Child Within* (Tucson: Zephyr Press, 1987), p. x.

3. You don't need a wardrobe mistress to create costumes. An Arab-type headdress can be made of an old pillowcase and rope. Long thin scarves worn over the head and wound around the shoulders are good for the "women." For small children, who particularly love to dress up, pillow cases with a hole cut in the top and slits made in the sides make good biblical robes—particularly if the pillow cases are striped. Avoid using bathrobes. "Animal" pajamas may be used for animal costumes. Look at pictures in Bible storybooks, leaflets, or reference books and be creative.

4. Walter Wink, *Transforming Bible Study*, 2nd ed. (Nashville: Abingdon Press, 1989), pp. 18-19.

4. "I Don't Do Pageants!"

1. See Thomas Emswiler and Sharon Neufer Emswiler, *Wholeness in Worship* (San Francisco: Harper & Row, 1980); Gwen Kennedy Neville and John H. Westerhoff III, *Learning Through Liturgy* (New York:

Seabury Press, 1983); David Ng and Virginia Thomas, *Children in the Worshiping Community* (Louisville: Westminster John Knox Press, 1981); Marjoris Morris, *Helping Children Feel at Home in Church* (Nashville: Discipleship Resources, 1988).

2. John H. Westerhoff III, *Will Our Children Have Faith?* (New York: Harper & Row, 1983), p. 56.

3. "Spirit of the Living God" with movements:

Spirit of the living God, (*begin with arms at sides, palms up, raise them over head, turn palms and face up on* God.)

Fall afresh on me! (*put tips of fingers together, bring arms down, end hands facing up*)

Repeat

Melt me! (*raise arms slightly above waist, then lower them with hands facing down.*)

Mold me! (*make a ball*)

Fill me! (*with palms facing up raise hand in front to shoulder level*)

Use me! (*extend arms out to side.*)

Spirit of the living God fall afresh on me (*repeat motions, holding the position for a time.*)

For words and music see Mary Hawkes and Paul Hamill, eds., *Sing to God* (New York: United Church Press, 1984) #57. Authorized adaptation by Word of God, Ann Arbor, Michigan. Copyright 1935, 1963. Moody Bible Institute of Chicago. Used by permission. This is a good source for special music for the church school.

4. Make a flannelgraph by mounting a piece of light-colored flannel (blue is particularly good—that way you've already got the sky) on a board approximately three feet square or larger. Put flannel on the back of pictures cut from old curricula and magazines—people, animals, trees, flowers, hills, streams, lakes, and what else can you think of. These flannel on the pictures will attach to the flannel on the board, allowing you to tell the story easily.

5. See Richard Avery and Donald Marsh, *The Great Parade* (Port Jervis, N.Y.: Proclamation Productions, 1971).

6. A Pentecost tree is made from a dead branch about five feet long with many little branches. Put it in a large flower pot with stones to hold it up. Decorate it with a red helium balloon at the top. Then give red, orange, and yellow crepe paper to the children and let them make flowers, flames, or whatever. If you happen to have Christmas tree candle holders that clip on, you can add red candles, but don't light them—that would create a fire hazard.

7. See Richard K. Avery and Donald S. Marsh, *The Avery and Marsh Song Book* (Port Jervis, N.Y.: Proclamation Productions, 1973).

8. For more on cooperative games, see Terry Orlick, *Cooperative Sports & Games Book: Challenge Without Competition* (New York: Pantheon Books, 1978).

9. Here is the prayer of confession we used:
Dear God, we are sorry that we
made a mess of our snacks sometimes;
have hurt animals;
throw garbage around;
cut down trees that we don't need;
hurt people;
hurt our bodies by smoking;
put pollutants in the air;
waste and pollute water.
We are sorry that we don't always listen;
don't obey our leaders;
don't do things we're supposed to do;
don't live in peace with others.
Forgive us, God, in Jesus' name, Amen.
Hear the Good News! In Jesus Christ we are forgiven.
Thanks be to God!

10. This adaptation of Psalm 8 was created by five students in grades three through six with my help. Two of the children were relatively unchurched. We stood on the stage in a semi-circle so we could see one another, and we created motions to express each line. Groups 1, 2, and 3 consisted of two persons each; groups 4 and 5 of three persons each. We began with the stagelights on and lights in the hall off.

Psalm 8
ALL: O Lord, Our Lord
1:       O How excellent
2:       Majestic
3:       OTerrific

ALL: Is your name in all the earth.
4:       Your glory above the heavens is chanted
5:       By the mouths of babes and infants
4:       You have founded a firmament because of your need
5:       To bring order out of chaos.

1:       When I look at the heavens
2:       The work of your fingers
3:       The moon and the stars which you have created

4:       What are we that you are aware of us

5:      And our possible humanity that you care for us?
4:      Yet you have made us little less than God
5:      And have given us the ability to be creative.

ALL: Let there be light!

(The lights in the hall come on.)

ALL: You have given us responsibility for all you have created.
LEADER: You have made us responsible for
1:          Domestic animals
2:          Wild animals
3:          The birds of the air
4:          The fish of the sea
5:          And whatever is moving in all creation.

ALL: O Lord, Our Lord
1:          How excellent
2:          Majestic
3:          Terrific
ALL: Is your name in all the earth!

Bibliography

Abrams, Jeremiah, ed. *Reclaiming the Inner Child.* Los Angeles: Jeremy P. Tarcher, 1990.

Anderson, Jill. *Thinking, Changing, Rearranging.* Eugene, Ore.: Timberlane Press, 1985.

———. *Improving Self Esteem in Young People.* Eugene, Ore.: Timberlane Press, 1981.

Avery, Richard K., and Donald S. Marsh. *The Avery and Marsh Song Book.* Port Jervis, N.Y.: Proclamation Productions, 1971.

———. *The Great Parade.* Port Jervis, N.Y.: Proclamation Productions, 1971.

Ban, Arlene J. *Teaching and Learning with Older Elementary Children.* New York: Judson Press, 1979.

Benzwie, Teresa. *A Moving Experience: Dance for Lovers of Children and the Child Within.* Tucson: Zephyr Press, 1987.

Bern, Patricia H., and Eve Bern. "Nurturing Succuss," *Pre-K Today.* New York: Scholastic, Inc., 1988.

Borysenko, Joan. *Guilt Is the Teacher, Love Is the Lesson.* New York: Warner Books, 1990.

———. *Minding the Body, Mending the Mind.* New York: Bantam Books, 1988.

Bredecamp, Sue, ed. "Developmentally Appropriate Practice in Early Childhood Programs Serving Children from Birth Through Age 8." *Young Children* (January 1988).

Brown, Robert McAfee. *The Bible Speaks to You.* Louisville: Westminster John Knox, 1985.

Caduto, Michael J., and Joseph Bruchac. *Keepers of the Earth: Native American Stories, with Environmental Activities for Children.* Golden, Colo.: Fulcrum, Inc., 1988.

Canfield, Jack and Harold Wells. *100 Ways to Enhance Self-concept in the Classrooom.* Englewood Cliffs, N.J.: Prentice-Hall, 1976.

Comstock, Sue. "Nurturing the Spiritual Experience of Children." *Church Educator* (February 1985).

Cully, Iris V. *Education for Spiritual Growth.* San Francisco: Harper & Row, 1984.

DUSO Kits: *Developing Understanding of Self and Others.* Circle Pines, Minn.: American Guidance Services, 1976.

Emswiler, Thomas Neufer, and Sharon Neufer Emswiler. *Wholeness in Worship.* San Francisco: Harper & Row, 1980.

Fowler, James W. *Becoming Adult, Becoming Christian: Adult Development and Christian Faith.* San Francisco: Harper & Row, 1984.
———. *Stages of Faith: The Psychology of Human Development and the Quest for Meaning.* San Francisco: Harper & Row, 1981.
Furnish, Dorothy Jean. *Experiencing the Bible with Children.* Nashville: Abingdon Press, 1990.

Gobbel, Roger A., and Gertrude G. Gobbel. *The Bible: A Child's Playground.* Philadelphia: Fortress Press, 1986.
Grady, Michael P. *Teaching and Brain Research: Guidelines for the Classroom.* New York: Longman, 1984.
Griggs, Donald. *Twenty New Ways of Teaching the Bible.* Nashville: Abingdon Press, 1979.
Griggs, Patricia. *Opening the Bible with Children: Beginning Bible Skills.* Nashville: Abingdon Press, 1986.

Hawes, Mary, and Paul Hamill, eds. *Sing to God.* New York: United Church Press, 1984.

Johnson, Susan. *Christian Spiritual Formation in the Church and Classroom.* Nashville: Abingdon Press, 1989.

Keating, Thomas. *The Heart of the World.* New York: Crossroads, 1981.
Kennett, Jiyu. *Zen Meditation.* Mt. Shasta: Shasta Abbey Press, 1980.
Kline, Peter. *The Everyday Genius: Restoring Children's Joy of Learning.* Arlington: Great Ocean Publishers, 1989.
Kohlberg, Lawrence. *The Philosophy of Moral Development.* San Francisco: Harper & Row, 1981.
Kostelnick, Marjorie J., Laura C. Stein, and Alice P. Whiren. "Children's Self-esteem: The Verbal Environment." *Childhood Education.* Association for Childhood Education International (Fall 1980).

Languis, Marlin. Tobie Sanders and Steven Tipps. *Brain and Learning: Directions in Early Childhood Education.* National Association for the Education of Young Children. Washington, DC. 1980.
Lein, Boyd. *Journey to Jerusalem.* Nashville: Abingdon Press, 1987.

L'Engle, Madeleine. *Trailing Clouds of Glory: Spiritual Values in Children's Books*. Louisville: Westminster John Knox, 1985.

LePage, Andy. *Transforming Education: The New Three R's*. Oakland, Calif.: Oakmore House Press, 1987.

McCarthy, Bernice. *The FourMat System: Teaching to Learning Styles with Right-Left Mode Techniques*. Barrington, Ill.: Excel, 1980.

Muro, James, and Don Dinkmeyer. *Counceling in the Elementary and Middle Schools: A Pragmatic Approach*. Dubuque: William C. Brown, 1987.

Neville, Gwen Kennedy, and John H. Westerhoff III. *Learning Through Liturgy*. New York: Seabury Press, 1983.

Ng, David, and Virginia Thomas. *Children in the Worshiping Community*. Louisville: Westminster John Knox Press, 1981.

Nouwen, Henri J. M. *The Wounded Healer*. Garden City, N.Y.: Doubleday, 1972.

Pagels, Elaine. *The Gnostic Gospels*. New York: Vantage Books, 1981.

Palmer, Parker. *The Promise of Paradox: A Celebration of Contradictions in the Christian Life*. Notre Dame: Ave Maria Press, 1980.

———. *To Know As We Are Known: A Spirituality of Education*. San Francisco: Harper & Row, 1983.

Rilke, Rainer Maria. *Letters to a Young Poet*. New York: W. W. Norton, 1954.

Rodegast, Pat, and Judith Stanton. *Emmanuel's Book*. New York: Bantam, 1987.

Runk, Lois M. *Working with Elementary Children*. Nashville: Discipleship Resources, 1990.

Russell, Joseph P. *Sharing Our Biblical Story: A Guide to Using Liturgical Readings as the Core of Church and Family Education*. Minneapolis: Winston Press, 1979.

Schmidt, Fran, and Alice Friedman. *Creative Conflict Solving for Kids*. Miami: Grace Contrino Abrams Peace Education Foundation, 1986.

———. *Fighting Fair for Kids*. Miami: Grace Contrino Abrams Peace Education Foundation, 1986.

Smith, Judy Gattis. *Developing a Child's Spiritual Growth Through Sight, Sound, Taste, Touch, and Smell*. Nashville: Abingdon Press, 1983.

———. *Teaching to Wonder: Spiritual Growth Through Imagination and Movement*. Nashville: Abingdon Press, 1989.

————. *Twenty-six Ways to Use Drama in Teaching the Bible.* Nashville: Abingdon Press, 1988.

Throckmorton, Burton H., Jr., ed. *Gospel Parallels: A Synopsis of the First Three Gospels.* Nashville: Thomas Nelson, 1979.

Vaughan, Frances. *Awakening Intuition.* Garden City, N.Y.: Doubleday, 1979.

————. *The Inward Arc: Healing and Wholeness in Psychotherapy and Spirituality.* Boston: Shambhala, 1986.

Westerhoff, John H. III. *Will Our Children Have Faith?* New York: Harper & Row, 1983.

Westerhoff, John H. III, and John D. Eusden. *The Spiritual Life: Learning East and West.* New York: Harper & Row, 1982.

Whitfield, Charles L. *Healing the Child Within.* Deerfield Beach: Health Communications, 1987.

Wink, Walter. *Transforming Bible Study.* 2nd ed. Nashville: Abingdon Press, 1990.

Winter, Paul. "Missa Gaia." Litchfield, Conn.: Living Music Records, Inc., 1982.